PATHWAYS

SECOND EDITION

Reading, Writing, and Critical Thinking

2

Teacher's Guide

CATHERINE MAZUR-JEFFERIES

NATIONAL
GEOGRAPHIC
L E A R N I N G

Australia • Brazil • Mexico • Singapore • United Kingdom • United States

Pathways Teacher's Guide 2,
Reading, Writing, and Critical Thinking,
Second Edition

Catherine Mazur-Jefferies

Publisher: Andrew Robinson

Executive Editor: Sean Bermingham

Associate Development Editor: Yvonne Tan

Director of Global Marketing: Ian Martin

Product Marketing Manager: Tracy Bailie

Media Researcher: Leila Hishmeh

Senior IP Analyst: Alexandra Ricciardi

IP Project Manager: Carissa Poweleit

Senior Director of Production: Michael Burggren

Senior Production Controller: Tan Jin Hock

Manufacturing Planner: Mary Beth Hennebury

Art Director: Brenda Carmichael

Compositor: MPS North America LLC

Cover Photo: Smoke rises from Manam Volcano off the coast of Papua New Guinea: © WENN Ltd/Alamy

For product information and technology assistance, contact us at
Cengage Learning Customer & Sales Support, cengage.com/contact

For permission to use material from this text or product,
submit all requests online at **cengage.com/permissions**
Further permissions questions can be emailed to
permissionrequest@cengage.com

ISBN-13: 978-1-337-62484-8

National Geographic Learning
20 Channel Center Street
Boston, MA 02210
USA

National Geographic Learning, a Cengage Learning Company, has a mission to bring the world to the classroom and the classroom to life. With our English language programs, students learn about their world by experiencing it. Through our partnerships with National Geographic and TED Talks, they develop the language and skills they need to be successful global citizens and leaders.

Locate your local office at **international.cengage.com/region**

Visit National Geographic Learning online at **NGL.Cengage.com/ELT**
Visit our corporate website at **www.cengage.com**

Printed in the United States of America

Print Number: 02   Print Year: 2018

CONTENTS

TEACHING WITH *PATHWAYS*

In *Pathways*, real-world content from *National Geographic* publications provides a context for meaningful language acquisition. Each unit's high-interest content is designed to motivate both students and teachers alike. Students will learn essential vocabulary, review important grammatical structures, and practice reading and writing skills that will allow them to succeed in academic settings.

The features in each unit of *Pathways Reading, Writing, and Critical Thinking* include:

• *Academic Skills* listing at the start of each unit that highlights the unit objectives
• *Explore the Theme* pages that introduce the unit theme and key vocabulary
• Authentic readings that present target vocabulary and provide ideas for writing
• Audio recordings of all the reading passages
• *Grammar References* that present key structures and language for writing assignments
• *Vocabulary Extension* exercises that can be used in class or for self-study and review

The *Pathways* series is designed to be used in a wide variety of language-learning programs, from high schools and community colleges, to private language institutes and intensive English programs. Pacing guides for implementing the program in various teaching situations are provided on page xii.

Teaching Academic Literacy

In addition to teaching essential English language reading and writing skills, the *Pathways* series promotes other aspects of academic literacy that will help students succeed in an academic setting, such as:

• Visual literacy
• Critical thinking
• Classroom participation and collaboration skills
• The ability to use technology for learning

Students build essential academic literacy skills while encountering stories about real people and places around the world. The use of high-interest content from *National Geographic* publications builds global and cultural awareness, and develops learners' understanding of important 21st century issues that affect us all.

Increasing Visual Literacy

In this digital age, the ability to process photographs, maps, charts, and graphs is essential. Most academic journals—both online and in print—present information with some kind of visual aid. Similarly, *Pathways* uses high quality infographics and photographs to help students develop the ability to interpret and discuss visual information.

STIMULATING INFOGRAPHICS from National Geographic publications help explain complex processes.

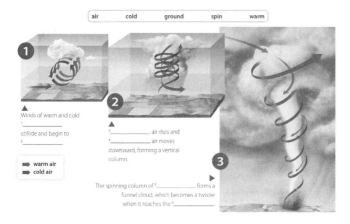

CHARTS, GRAPHS, AND TIMELINES present information visually.

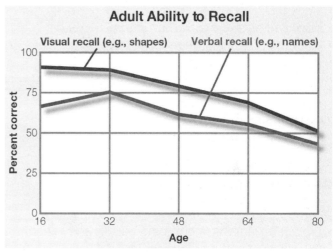

MAPS show locations and geographical features, and illustrate historical facts and current trends.

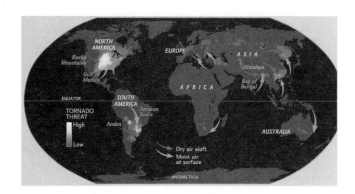

GRAPHIC ORGANIZERS show the relationships between ideas in a visual way.

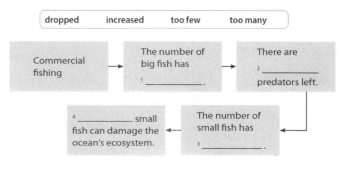

Using Videos

Pathways uses videos from National Geographic's award-winning film collection. The videos present a visually dynamic perspective of each unit's theme. Each video's narration has been carefully graded to match student proficiency levels.

Teaching Video Viewing Skills

Pathways promotes visual and digital literacy so learners can competently use a wide range of modern media. Videos differ from reading texts in important ways. Because students are processing more than just words, extra layers of meaning need to be understood:

- Information about the video's setting
- Signs and captions identifying people or places
- Maps and diagrams explaining information and processes
- Nonverbal communication such as facial expressions, gestures, and body language
- Music and sound effects

The transcripts for the videos can be found in the Teacher's Guide on pages 101–106.

The Video Section

Each unit features activities for students to do before, while, and after watching the video.

BEFORE VIEWING

This section provides background knowledge and stimulates interest in the topic by:

- predicting video content using images and captions.
- providing a short reading passage that includes background information about the topic.
- pre-teaching vocabulary from the video.

WHILE VIEWING

As they watch the video, students focus on:

- checking their predictions.
- identifying main ideas.
- watching and listening for particular details.
- inferring opinions and attitudes.

AFTER VIEWING

Students check their comprehension and relate the video to other aspects of the unit by:

- applying the ideas in the videos to their own lives and communities.
- synthesizing information from the video and information from the reading passages.

Building Critical Thinking Skills

Students today are expected to do more than just learn and memorize information. The ability to think critically about a topic—to analyze, evaluate, and apply ideas—is increasingly essential in an academic setting. *Pathways* actively fosters critical thinking while students read, listen, write, and discuss.

Critical Thinking and Language

Critical thinking requires a deep processing of language, which aids language acquisition. Articulating complex responses requires creative thought and word associations, which lead to better comprehension and retention of target language.

These are some of the critical thinking skills covered in *Pathways*:

- **Analyzing** Examining a text in close detail in order to identify key points, similarities, and differences.
- **Applying** Deciding how ideas or information might be relevant in a different context e.g., applying possible solutions to problems.
- **Evaluating** Using evidence to decide how relevant, important, or useful something is. This involves, for example, looking carefully at the sources of information, or the reasons the writer provides for or against something.
- **Inferring** "Reading between the lines;" in other words, identifying what a writer is saying indirectly, or implicitly, rather than directly, or explicitly.
- **Synthesizing** Gathering appropriate information and ideas from more than one source and making a judgment, summary, or conclusion based on the evidence.
- **Reflecting** Relating ideas and information in a text to your own personal experience and viewpoints, and forming your own opinion.

Each unit contains several opportunities for critical thinking. There is also an expanded *Critical Thinking* task in one of the *Understanding the Reading* sections:

> **CRITICAL THINKING**   When you **evaluate evidence**, you decide if it supports the writer's claims. Consider whether the evidence is *relevant* (does it relate to the main idea?), *logical* (does it make sense?), and *sufficient* (does it give enough support for the idea?).

C Look at the chart in exercise B again. Then discuss the questions below with a partner.

1. In your opinion, does the fossil evidence help support each theory about feathers? Do you see a clear link?
2. Do you think the writer gives enough fossil evidence and modern-day examples for each theory?
3. Which theory about feathers do you find most or least convincing? Why?

CRITICAL THINKING:
EVALUATING
EVIDENCE

Frequently Asked Questions

How are the Student Book units organized?

Each unit consists of four main sections:

Reading 1, Video, Reading 2, Writing

The unit opens with an introduction to the unit theme. The reading passages and videos that follow, together with their corresponding exercises, build towards a final writing task that incorporates the skills, topics, and language presented in the unit.

Will my students be able to handle the themes in the book?

The content and language is graded so that students can come into the series with little or no background information.

Each unit starts with a *Think and Discuss* page. The questions get students thinking about the unit's theme. The *Explore the Theme* spread then formally introduces students to the theme. It makes use of short passages, statistics, infographics, and other images to ease students in.

As students progress through a unit, exercises and activities add further to students' knowledge of the theme. By the time students get to the writing task, they will have enough language and information to express in writing their own ideas about the topic.

How are *Readings 1* and *2* related?

The two readings offer different perspectives on the unit theme. They usually consist of contrasting text types, for example, one might be an explanatory magazine-type article with infographics, and the other an adapted interview. The variety of text types is designed to mirror the range of reading texts that learners will encounter in print and online.

How does the series build vocabulary skills?

Each reading passage contains eight to ten high-frequency vocabulary items (highlighted in blue). These are introduced in the *Preparing to Read* section, which focuses on developing students' ability to use contextual clues to determine meaning. Target words are then reinforced and recycled throughout subsequent units. In addition, *Vocabulary Extension* activities at the end of the Student Book expand on some of these target words by introducing useful collocations, highlighting different word forms, and presenting common prefixes, suffixes, and word roots.

How are reading and writing integrated in the series?

All of the sections and exercises in each unit are thematically linked. *Readings 1* and *2* and their corresponding activities present and reinforce ideas, vocabulary, and grammar that students will use in their *Writing Task*. For example, students may learn to understand pronoun reference in *Reading 1*, and then be taught to use pronouns to avoid repetition as part of the *Writing Task*. Or students may read about explorers in both reading passages, and then be asked to write about a place they would like to explore.

What is the writing process approach taken in this series?

Students learn early on that writing is re-writing. This is the premise of *Pathways'* process approach to writing. As students work through the pre-writing, writing, and post-writing activities in each unit, they draft and re-draft their assignments. By repeating this process as they progress through the units, students internalize the steps and gradually become more independent writers.

How does *Pathways* develop writing skills?

At the end of every unit, students complete a *Writing Task*. In Level 2, students develop their ability to write a wide range of paragraphs, including opinion, summary, and comparison paragraphs.

A section called *Exploring Written English* helps to prepare students for the *Writing Task*, and contains the following features:

- The *Language for Writing* box highlights lexical or grammar points that are useful for that unit's writing task. Examples include using the simple past for describing historical events and using expressions like *even though* and *although* to make concessions.
- The *Writing Skill* box teaches useful paragraph-level writing skills. Early units explain simpler concepts like writing strong topic and concluding sentences. Subsequent units include more advanced paragraph writing skills such as how to structure a comparison paragraph.

The *Exploring Written English* section gives students the tools they need for their writing task, which they will perform in five stages:

Brainstorming, Planning, Drafting, Revising, Editing

Students are guided through these steps, working through a series of activities to help shape, structure, and fine-tune their writing. The *Revising* and *Editing* stages each include a guided practice task, using model examples. Students learn how to apply the principles in these practice tasks to their own writing.

The *MyELT* online workbook provides additional guided writing tasks that build on the skills and language that learners have developed in the Student Book unit.

Instructors may wish to refer to the Writing Assessment Rubric in the Teacher's Guide when assessing students' written work, or provide students with a copy of the rubric for them to do a peer assessment of their final drafts.

Pathways Reading, Writing, and Critical Thinking 2: Writing Assessment Rubric

Name: _____   Unit: _____

Criterion	Score of 4	Score of 3	Score of 2	Score of 1
Pre-writing and organization	☐ **Well organized** • Clear topic sentence • Supporting ideas are in a logical sequence • Strong concluding sentence	☐ **Good organization** • Clear topic sentence • Supporting ideas are in a mostly logical sequence • Good concluding sentence	☐ **Some organization** • Topic sentence is slightly unclear • Sequencing of supporting ideas is unclear • Weak concluding sentence	☐ **Lacks organization** • Weak topic sentence or lack of a topic sentence • Lack of sequencing of supporting ideas • No concluding sentence
Content	☐ **Excellent supporting ideas that are appropriate to the task** • Supporting ideas are well explained and have enough details • Supporting ideas are related to the task goal and the paragraph's main idea	☐ **Strong supporting ideas that are appropriate to the task** • Supporting ideas are somewhat explained with a bit of detail • Supporting ideas are mostly related to the task goal and the paragraph's main idea	☐ **Good supporting ideas, but some are slightly unrelated to the task** • Supporting ideas are incomplete with little detail • Some supporting ideas are unrelated to the task or the paragraph's main idea	☐ **Weak supporting ideas or ideas that are unrelated to the task** • Supporting ideas are weak with little or no detail • Supporting ideas are unrelated to the task or the paragraph's main idea
Vocabulary	☐ **Wide range of vocabulary** • Appropriate and related to task • Effective use of less common words • Errors are minor and not frequent	☐ **Good range of vocabulary** • Appropriate and related to task • Good attempt to use less common words • Occasional errors, but meaning is still clear	☐ **Average range of vocabulary** • Mostly appropriate and related to task • Some attempt to use less common words • A number of errors that affect understanding	☐ **Limited range of vocabulary** • Minimally appropriate and related to task • Inaccurate use of target vocabulary • Frequent errors that greatly affect understanding
Sentence Structure and Grammar	☐ **Excellent sentence structure and language use** • Varied sentence structure • Very few grammatical errors in subject-verb agreement, verb tense agreement, use of conjunctions, etc.	☐ **Good sentence structure and language use** • Good variety of sentence structure • A few grammatical errors in subject-verb agreement, verb tense agreement, use of conjunctions, etc. that do not affect understanding	☐ **Average sentence structure and language use** • Little variety in sentence structure • A number of grammatical errors in subject-verb agreement, verb tense agreement, use of conjunctions, etc. that slightly affect understanding	☐ **Weak sentence structure and language use** • Simple or repetitive sentence structure • Many grammatical errors in subject-verb agreement, verb tense agreement, use of conjunctions, etc. that greatly affect understanding

Spelling and Punctuation	☐ **Excellent command of spelling and punctuation**
	• Few or no spelling errors
	• Correct use of punctuation:
	  ○ Capitalization of names and places and at the beginning of sentences
	  ○ Use of comma between clauses and where appropriate
	  ○ Use of period or question mark at the end of sentences
	  ○ Use of apostrophes for indicating possession
		☐ **Good command of spelling and punctuation**
		• Some spelling errors, but mostly with uncommon words
		• Mostly correct use of punctuation:
		  ○ Capitalization of names and places and at the beginning of sentences
		  ○ Use of comma between clauses and where appropriate
		  ○ Use of period or question mark at the end of sentences
		  ○ Use of apostrophes for indicating possession
			☐ **Average command of spelling and punctuation**
			• A number of spelling errors, some with common words
			• Some incorrect use of punctuation:
			  ○ Capitalization of names and places and at the beginning of sentences
			  ○ Use of comma between clauses and where appropriate
			  ○ Use of period or question mark at the end of sentences
			  ○ Use of apostrophes for indicating possession
				☐ **Weak command of spelling and punctuation**
				• Many spelling errors
				• Largely incorrect use of punctuation:
				  ○ Capitalization of names and places and at the beginning of sentences
				  ○ Use of comma between clauses and where appropriate
				  ○ Use of period or question mark at the end of sentences
				  ○ Use of apostrophes for indicating possession

Score				

Total score: ☐ / 20

USING THE TEACHER'S GUIDE

Each unit of this Teacher's Guide contains:

- Overviews of reading passages and videos
- Background information and key lesson points
- Teaching notes for each exercise
- Answer keys
- Follow-up questions and activities

Other features include:

Recommended Time Frames

Look out for the small clock icon with recommended times for completing various tasks. While the recommended total time required for each unit is about five class hours, this will of course vary depending on your particular teaching situation. Likewise, the time allocated for specific sections should be used more as a guide than as a rule. Refer to the pacing guides on the following page for a more detailed breakdown.

Ideas for...EXPANSION

These contain suggestions for extra classroom activities that can be used when students need additional support, or when there is an opportunity to explore a different aspect of the unit theme.

In addition, this Teacher's Guide also contains:

Video Transcripts

Use these for a more detailed study of the video content. The scripts, for example, can be provided to students after they view the video as additional reading practice.

Graphic Organizers

There is a photocopiable graphic organizer for one of the reading passages in the unit. The organizers include concept maps, process diagrams, and note-taking charts that can be handed out to students before or after they read the passage, to help them organize key points.

PACING GUIDES

One unit of *Pathways* typically requires 4.5–5 hours to complete. All ten units require approximately 45–50 hours.

By setting aside portions of each unit as homework, or by using extension activities and ancillaries, a *Pathways* unit can be adapted to suit various course durations. Here are some examples:

Total course length: 45 hours	Total course length: 60 hours	Total course length: 90 hours	Total course length: 120 hours
30-week course: 1 × 90 minute class per week	**30-week course:** 2 × 60 min classes per week **15-week course:** 4 × 60 min classes per week	**30-week course:** 2 × 90 min classes per week	**30-week course:** 4 × 60 min classes per week
1 unit = 3 classes (4.5 hours) 10 units = 30 classes	1 unit = 5 classes (5 hours) 10 units = 50 classes (out of 60 classes total) Remaining time = 10 hours *(Presentations / exams / reviews / school vacations)*	1 unit = 4 classes (6 hours) 10 units = 40 classes (out of 60 classes total) Remaining time = 30 hours *(group projects / presentations / exams / reviews / school vacations)*	1 unit = 8 classes (8 hours) 10 units = 80 classes (out of 120 classes total) Remaining time = 40 hours *(group projects / presentations / exams / reviews / school vacations)*
Class 1: Think and Discuss Explore the Theme Preparing to Read Reading 1 Understanding the Reading **Class 2:** Developing Reading Skills Video Preparing to Read Reading 2 **Class 3:** Understanding the Reading Exploring Written English Writing Task Unit Review	**Class 1:** Think and Discuss Explore the Theme Preparing to Read Reading 1 **Class 2:** Understanding the Reading Developing Reading Skills **Class 3:** Video Preparing to Read (vocabulary tasks) **Class 4:** Preparing to Read (predicting) Reading 2 Understanding the Reading **Class 5:** Exploring Written English Writing Task Unit Review	**Class 1:** Think and Discuss Explore the Theme Preparing to Read Reading 1 Understanding the Reading **Class 2:** Developing Reading Skills Video Preparing to Read Reading 2 **Class 3:** Understanding the Reading Exploring Written English **Class 4:** Writing Task Unit Review Extension activities	**Class 1:** Think and Discuss Explore the Theme Preparing to Read Reading 1 **Class 2:** Understanding the Reading Developing Reading Skills **Class 3:** Video **Class 4:** Preparing to Read Reading 2 **Class 5:** Understanding the Reading **Class 6:** Exploring Written English **Class 7:** Writing task Unit Review **Class 8:** Extension activities / group projects
This option assumes that: – the first draft, and the revising and editing of drafts, are set as homework.	This option assumes that: – the first draft, and the revising and editing of drafts, are set as homework.	This option assumes that: There is enough time to complete the entire Student Book and extension activities / Ideas for Expansion in class. – The Teacher's Guide provides numerous follow-up questions and extension activities in each unit. – Online Workbook activities and ExamView unit quizzes can be set as homework.	This option assumes that: There is enough time to complete the entire Student Book and extension activities / Ideas for Expansion in class. – The Teacher's Guide contains numerous follow-up questions and extension activities. – Online Workbook activities and ExamView unit quizzes can be done in class or set as homework.

HAPPINESS

ACADEMIC TRACK
Health Science / Sociology

ACADEMIC SKILLS

READING	Identifying the main idea
WRITING	Writing a strong topic sentence
GRAMMAR	Review of the simple present tense
CRITICAL THINKING	Inferring meaning

UNIT OVERVIEW

The theme of this unit is happiness, and the different factors that contribute to happiness around the world are explored. The unit also discusses longevity studies and explores ways to become a happier person.

- **READING 1:** This reading describes life in Mexico and Singapore and the diverse factors that lead to happiness.

- **VIDEO:** The video provides a look at centenarians around the world and the reasons certain groups of people, most notably those in Okinawa, Japan, are living longer.

- **READING 2:** This reading discusses six factors associated with happiness and gives examples of how to enhance these areas in one's own life.

Students draw on what they've read and watched to write an opinion paragraph evaluating happiness in their own communities. The unit prepares them by introducing vocabulary to talk about happiness, reviewing the simple present tense, and offering tips for writing strong topic sentences. The unit also explains how to identify the main idea of a paragraph. Lastly, it introduces students to brainstorming and using an outline to prepare drafts—skills that students will use in every unit's *Writing Task*.

THINK AND DISCUSS *(page 1)*

The questions help prepare students for the subject matter covered in the unit—happiness around the world. The scene depicts children playing on swings made of rope in a vehicle (a jeepney) in the Philippines.
- Have students study the picture, title, and captions.
- Discuss the photo as a class. Ask students to describe what they see. Ask: Why do you think they are happy? Do you think children are happier than adults? Have students explain their answers.

- Discuss the two questions as a class. For question **1**, write the word *happy* on the board, and create a word web with student answers (relaxed, loved). For question **2**, have volunteers share their answers. Ask the class what characteristics they notice happy people share.

ANSWER KEY

THINK AND DISCUSS

Answers will vary. Possible answers:

1. Happiness can mean different things to different people. I think true happiness is when you are surrounded by people who love you and you feel fulfilled in your life.
2. My friend Janna is someone who seems happy. She likes to laugh and be around other people. She always looks on the positive side of a situation, even when times are tough.

EXPLORE THE THEME *(pages 2–3)*

The opening spread provides information and statistics about the happiest countries in the world, according to the World Database of Happiness.
- Allow time for students to study the spread and answer the questions in part A individually. Elicit meanings of *rate* and *on a scale of one to ten*.
- Discuss answers as a class. Ask students why they think these countries were chosen and whether the statistics described in the spread reflect their own experiences.
- Have students answer the question in part **B**. Remind students to use the correct forms of the words.
- Elicit example sentences from students for each of the blue words.

ANSWER KEY

EXPLORE THE THEME

A   Answers will vary. Possible answers:

1. Yes, I've been to Canada and Mexico. Most of the countries shown here are very scenic and have stunning natural views, so maybe that's why people from these countries are generally happy.
2. Many countries have high GDPs, but then again, number 1 (Costa Rica) and number 3 (Mexico) don't, so that can't be the major reason for happiness. I think this suggests that there are other factors that contribute to happiness.

B   provide; secure; standard of living

Reading 1

30 MINS **PREPARING TO READ** *(page 4)*

A Building Vocabulary

Building Vocabulary exercises introduce students to key vocabulary items from the reading passage. Students should find the blue words in the passage and use contextual clues to guess the meanings of the words. One useful clue is part of speech. For example: Nouns are often preceded by articles such as *a* or *the* (*a team*, *the project*); verbs often take the infinitive form and follow the word *to* (*to produce*, *to communicate*); adjectives frequently appear after forms of the verb *be* (*normal*, *extraordinary*). Recognizing parts of speech can help students understand new words better.

- Have students complete the exercise individually.
- Check answers as a class. Ask students for the part of speech of each blue word. What other clues from the reading passage did students find helpful?
- Elicit example sentences for each vocabulary item.

See Vocabulary Extension 1A on page 203 of the Student Book for additional practice with Word Partners: Expressions with living.

B Using Vocabulary

Students should practice using the new vocabulary items while answering the three questions.

- Have students work in pairs to answer the questions.
- Check answers as a class. Elicit example answers from students. For question **1**, ask students how often they socialize with their classmates. For question **2**, do students think their lists of basic necessities are the same as they would be if they had lived 100 years ago? For question **3**, what do they think could be done about poverty in their countries?

Ideas for... EXPANSION

A vocabulary notebook is a great way for students to build their vocabularies. Demonstrate on the board how to write new words in the notebook, and include details such as *part of speech, meaning, translation*, and an *example sentence*. (Example: *socialize (verb): To spend time with other people for fun. I like to socialize with my classmates during our lunch break.*)

C Brainstorming

Have students list things that they think they need to be happy. Each idea should be brief. Elicit one or two examples before students begin (family, football).

- Have students work individually to complete the exercise.
- Have them compare answers in pairs. Encourage students to explain *why* they chose their answers.
- Elicit example answers from the class. On the board, create a word web with students' answers.

D Predicting

Predicting helps the reader understand a passage better later. Here, students should read the title and subheads and make their own guesses about this reading.

- Have students read the title and subheads. Stress that students should not try to read the entire passage. You may want to give a time limit of 1 to 2 minutes.
- Have them discuss their answers in pairs.
- Discuss the most probable answer as a class. Revisit this question after completing the reading.

ANSWER KEY

PREPARING TO READ

A 1. socialize

2. poverty (Note: *Social programs* are ways to help people in a community with childcare, after-school programs, or care for the elderly, etc.)

3. access (Note: *Access* often appears in the phrase *have access to*: Many people have access to the Internet through smartphones.)

4. financial (Note: *Concerned* means worried.)

5. equal

6. Freedom (Note: *Freedom of speech* means that citizens have the right to voice their opinions.)

7. basic necessities (Note: *A struggle* is something that is very difficult to do.)

B Answers will vary. Possible answers:

1. my classmates and my family

2. access to healthcare, freedom

3. Yes, money is not equally distributed in my country. Some people are very wealthy, but many are very poor. The government is trying to tackle this problem by setting a national minimum wage.

C Answers will vary. Possible answers: health, friends, an interesting job, money, family, a safe environment

D b (Note: This passage doesn't talk about how to measure happiness or whether one country is the happiest. It discusses how different things contribute to happiness, so b is the correct answer.)

1.01 Have students read the passage individually, or play the audio and have students read along.

OVERVIEW OF THE READING

The passage presents two contrasting case studies, Singapore and Mexico, which help to make the point that there is no single reason that people are happy. Work, security, safety, freedom, and socializing with friends and family all play important roles.

Online search terms: Happy Planet Index; World Happiness Report

UNDERSTANDING THE READING
(page 7)

40 MINS

A Understanding the Main Idea

Students are asked to identify the main idea of the reading passage.

- Have students complete the activity individually.
- Check the answer as a class. Ask students how they arrived at their answers. Introduce the technique of using a process of elimination.

B Understanding Details

Students test their understanding of the details in the passage by indicating whether the statements are true for Mexico, Singapore, or both. Ask students to write the letter corresponding to the sentence in each circle. Draw the diagram on the board, and demonstrate with the first sentence. (Example: Sentence a is true for both Mexico and Singapore.)

- Allow students time to complete the diagram individually.
- Have them check their answers in pairs.
- Draw the diagram on the board, and discuss answers as a class.

C Critical Thinking: Inferring Meaning

The *Critical Thinking* box explains how to guess the meaning of words by using context. You would have covered this with students already in *Preparing to Read*, but go over the lesson again because inferring meaning is a useful skill that will be practiced throughout the book. Ask why inferring meaning can be better than using a dictionary. Explain that stopping to look up a word halfway through a passage can affect reading fluency and interfere with comprehension. Exercise **C** offers students more practice with this skill, this time with more challenging words. Students need to locate the words in the reading and pay close attention to the words around them.

- Have students complete the task individually.
- Check answers as a class. Ask students how they arrived at their answers. Elicit example sentences for each word.

D Critical Thinking: Justifying Your Opinion

Students should use what they have learned to justify their opinions. Remind students that in their daily lives, they are often asked to give reasons for their opinions. (Example: On the board, write: *We have the best English class*. Point out that before believing this, people will want to know the reasons. Elicit reasons: *Because the students are friendly; the book is engaging, etc.*)

- Have students complete the task individually.
- Have students discuss their answers in pairs.
- Discuss answers as a class. Elicit example answers.

Ideas for… **EXPANSION**

To supplement exercise **D**, have students discuss whether their country (or region) is more like Singapore or Mexico. Does it have elements of both? Remind students to justify their reasons, using *because* to support each statement. Have students make a T-chart (dividing the paper vertically into two sections) to create a list of ways that their country is similar to Singapore and Mexico. Then compare T-charts with the rest of the class.

ANSWER KEY

UNDERSTANDING THE READING

A a (Option b is not mentioned in the reading passage. Option c is incorrect because some people in Mexico don't have a safe or secure life but are still happy.)

B
Mexico	d
Singapore	b, e
Both	a, c

C 1. look after
   2. strict
   3. decent
   4. happy medium

D Answers will vary. Possible answers: I think I would prefer to live in Mexico because I wouldn't feel comfortable in a place with very strict rules. *Or* I think I would prefer to live in Singapore because I think it's very important to feel safe and secure.

⏱20 MINS DEVELOPING READING SKILLS *(page 8)*

Reading Skill: Identifying the Main Idea

The *Reading Skill* box explains that the main idea of a reading is what the writer wants readers to understand about a topic. It's important to be able to determine the main idea so that students can understand the general meaning of a passage. Ask students to read the text in the *Reading Skill* box. When they have finished, tell students to close their books. Ask them what the reading was about. Elicit: *Mexico, sun, happy*. Now have students open their books again and read the statements. Working as a class, they should see that sentence c is the main idea; the other two sentences provide supporting details.

A Matching

Each of the sentences is a main idea for one of the paragraphs in the reading. Explain that students should read and match the paragraphs to the main ideas.

- Allow time for students to complete the task individually.
- Have students check answers in pairs.
- Discuss answers as a class.

B Identifying the Main Idea

Students read the paragraph about Denmark. If possible, point out the location of Denmark on a map. Ask students if they think people there will be happy or not. Ask them to justify their reasons.

- Allow students time to read the paragraph and write the main idea individually.
- Have them compare their answers in pairs.
- Discuss answers as a class. If time permits, ask volunteers to write their answers on the board, and ask students to discuss what makes a good main idea sentence.

ANSWER KEY

DEVELOPING READING SKILLS

A **1.** C; **2.** G; **3.** F; **4.** H; **5.** D

B Answers will vary. Possible answer: Being healthy makes people feel happier.

Video

⏱40 MINS VIEWING: LONGEVITY LEADERS *(pages 9–10)*

Overview of the Video

The video discusses the factors that enable people to live to be 100 years old. The video describes how the number of elderly people in the world is growing, and it investigates factors that enable people to live to a very old age. Two of the places it focuses on are Sardinia, Italy, and Okinawa, Japan.

Online search terms: Sardinia centenarians; Okinawa diet

BEFORE VIEWING

A Predicting

Predicting the video content helps students understand it better when they view it. The title suggests that this is about people who live a long time. The photograph shows that elderly people, such as this shepherd, can still lead active lifestyles. The caption reinforces this, stating that the man in Sardinia still works outside. Students might infer that the video will be about people around the world who live a long time.

- Allow some time for students to study the title, photo, and captions.
- Discuss as a class. On the board, write the words "long life," and make a word web with students' ideas. Ask students: Do they know anyone over 100 years old? What is the secret to living a long life?

B Learning About the Topic

The paragraph prepares students for the video by giving them background information about the links between living a long time and being happy.

- Have students complete the task individually.
- Discuss answers as a class. Elicit example answers. Ask students whether they agree with these findings. Would they follow this guide to live a longer life?

C Vocabulary in Context

This exercise introduces students to some of the key words used in the video.

- Have students complete the task individually.
- Check answers as a class. Elicit example sentences for each word. Remind students to use the *inferring meaning from context* skills that they learned earlier in the unit. Ask: What is the part of speech for each of these words? What are the clues that helped to determine the meanings?

ANSWER KEY

BEFORE VIEWING

A Answers will vary. Possible answers:

They eat healthy food; they stay active; they have hobbies; they have a positive attitude; they have families that take care of them.

B 1. eat healthy foods; exercise; have a positive outlook

2. Answers will vary. Possible answers: When people are unhappy, the stress can cause them to lose sleep and not take care of themselves. This can affect their health. When people are happy, they are more likely to be healthier.

C 1. traditional lifestyle

2. centenarian (Note: The root of this word, *cent*, means 100. One hundred years is a century, percent is a number divided by 100, and 100 cents make a U.S. dollar.)

3. processed food

WHILE VIEWING

A ▶ Understanding the Main Idea

Have students read the items silently before you play the video.
- Have them complete the task while the video is playing.
- Check the answer as a class. Discuss why the other statements are incorrect.

B ▶ Understanding Details

Have students read the questions and write any answers they recall from the first viewing before playing the video a second time.
- Have students complete the task while the video is playing.
- Check answers as a class. Ask students whether any facts in the video surprised them.

ANSWER KEY

WHILE VIEWING

A c (Note: The narrator in the video talks about an aging population, but he doesn't mention a struggle (option a). Happiness (option b) is not mentioned as the most important factor. Both medicine and lifestyle choices are mentioned, so c is the correct answer.)

B 1. People are living longer.

2. Answers will vary. Possible answers: whales—200 + years; giant tortoises—150 + years; elephants—up to 70 years

3. Answers will vary. Possible answers: They stay active, have hobbies, eat locally grown food, have access to good medical care, and keep their friends and family close.

4. They eat more processed foods and may be less active.

AFTER VIEWING

A Reacting to the Video

Students are asked to reflect on the information in the video and relate it to their own lives.
- Have students discuss question **1** in pairs. Ask students: How are the elderly treated in their community? Who takes care of the elderly in their community?
- Have students analyze the quote in question **2** in pairs. Ask *why* they think this has changed from how scientists viewed aging in the past.
- Ask for volunteers to share their answers.

B Critical Thinking: Synthesizing

Students draw on information from both Reading 1 and the Video to *synthesize* their answers. Ask students to skim through Reading 1 again to refresh their memories.
- Allow students time to answer the questions in pairs.
- Discuss as a class. Elicit example answers, and write them on the board.

> **Ideas for… EXPANSION**
>
> Have students work in groups of three or four to create a pamphlet (online or on paper) with advice for people who want to live longer. Encourage students to use both the information from the video and their own ideas. Have students share their pamphlets with the class.

ANSWER KEY

AFTER VIEWING

Answer will vary. Possible answers:

A 1. There are many elderly people in my community. I think this is because we have very good medical care here and a healthy environment.

2. I think this means that some people think of aging as a bad thing, so scientists are trying to find ways to prevent or delay the effects of aging.

B Singapore; they have access to good medical care.

Mexico; they have the support of their families.

Reading 2

 PREPARING TO READ *(page 11)*

A Building Vocabulary

In this exercise, students complete sentences that follow the same topic as the reading passage. Point out that students need to use the correct forms of the words. Ask students to use contextual clues from the passage to infer the meanings of the words, if necessary.

• Have students complete the exercise individually.
• Check answers as a class. Elicit example sentences for each vocabulary item.

See Vocabulary Extension 1B on page 203 of the Student Book for additional practice with Word Forms: Words as Nouns and Verbs.

B Using Vocabulary

Students should use the new vocabulary items while discussing the two questions.

• Have students work in pairs to answer the questions.
• Discuss answers as a class. Elicit example answers from students.

C Brainstorming

This exercise gets students thinking about factors associated with happiness, the topic of the reading passage. Ideas should be brief. Remind students of the word web that the class created earlier in the unit, or draw the web on the board with a sample answer.

• Allow time for students to skim through the reading for the four factors. Students should write their answers individually.
• Have students check their answers as a class.
• Have students work in pairs to add words or phrases that relate to each of the four factors. Provide one or two examples, if necessary.
• Ask for volunteers to share their answers, and write the words and phrases on a word web on the board.

ANSWER KEY

PREPARING TO READ

A
1. long-term
2. communities; support
3. well-being
4. volunteered; grateful
5. mood; factors

B Answers will vary. Possible answers:
1. My community is very safe and clean, but people don't talk to their neighbors so it can be lonely if you don't already have friends.
2. fun friends; exercise; shopping; vacations

C Answers will vary. Possible answers:
Stay Connected—family; friends; Skype.
Keep Active—exercise; walk; sports.
Buy Less—recycle; reuse; save money.
Give Away—donate; volunteer; help others.

 1.02 Have students read the passage individually, or play the audio and have students read along.

OVERVIEW OF THE READING

The reading passage identifies four common factors - staying connected, keeping active, buying less, and giving things (or time) away - that can affect everyone's happiness. It suggests that paying attention to these four factors will make you happier and are not difficult to do, either! A number of experts explain their findings in this article, including a psychiatrist, a designer, an author, and a social science researcher.

Online search terms: Nic Marks; Michael Norton TED Talk; live happier

UNDERSTANDING THE READING *(page 14)*

A Understanding the Main Idea

Students choose a sentence that summarizes the content of the passage.

• Have students complete the task individually.
• Check answers as a class. Ask students where they found their answers.

B Identifying Main Ideas

Students read the six scenarios and check the four that follow the advice in the reading passage.

• Allow time for students to complete the task individually.
• Check answers as a class. Ask students which section of advice in the reading passage matches with each correct scenario.

C Critical Thinking: Inferring Meaning

Go over the *Critical Thinking* box that appears earlier in the unit with students again. Students should use contextual clues from the passage to figure out what the words mean. As a class, have students find the first bold phrase in the reading. As a class, elicit the meaning from the context.

- Allow time for students to complete the rest of the task individually.
- Check answers as a class.
- Ask students: When people want to *take the focus off* themselves, what do they usually do? How do you know when someone has low *self-esteem*? How will learning English *enrich* your life? What's a job with a very high *salary*?

D Critical Thinking: Reflecting

Explain that connecting a reading with their own lives helps students interact with the material and enhances their language learning skills. Have a student read the sample answer aloud.

- Allow students time to answer the questions individually.
- Have students share their answers with a partner.
- Discuss as a class. Elicit example answers.

ANSWER KEY

UNDERSTANDING THE READING

A b (Note: The answer, b, is found in the first paragraph. Option a is incorrect because the passage is not about different types of people, and option c is incorrect because the author doesn't say that forming social connections is the most important factor.)

B 1, 2, 4, and 6 (Note: Scenario 1 is an example of buying less; Scenario 2 is an example of keeping active; Scenario 4 is an example of giving away; and Scenario 6 is an example of staying connected.)

C 1. confident
2. money
3. better
4. less

D Answers will vary. Possible answers:

1. Stay Connected—I can invite friends to dinner once a week, and try to see relatives who live far away as often as possible.

2. Give Away—I can donate clothes that I don't wear anymore to local charities. Maybe I can even volunteer at the charity thrift store.

3. Buy Less—If I go to the mall less often, I won't buy as much. Maybe I can meet my friends at a museum or in a park instead of at the shopping mall.

Ideas for... EXPANSION

Ask students to imagine that aliens have landed on Earth, and they want to learn about this thing called "happiness." What would students tell them about happiness? Have students work in groups of three or four to create a list of four factors as a word web. Each group should write these either on paper or on the board and compare their answers with those from the rest of the class. The class can vote to determine which list to submit to the aliens.

Ideas for... EXPANSION

Point out to students that Reading 2 had a lot of quotes from different experts. Ask students why they think the author decided to include these quotes. Explain how to use quotation marks and attribute a quote to a person. If computers are available, have students search online for famous quotes about happiness. Have students choose one quote and write it on a piece of paper, with the name of the person as well. Then ask students to share their quotes with the class. Have students explain why they chose their quotes, and what the quote means to them.

Writing

OVERVIEW

In this section, students prepare to write their first full paragraphs. The lesson starts by teaching students the difference between facts and routines. Students then review the simple present tense through several activities. Students learn how to write a strong topic sentence. In the *Writing Task*, students apply these lessons by brainstorming, planning, and writing about happiness in their community. As added support, they will encounter two drafts of sample paragraphs and revising strategies that the author used. Students will use a checklist to revise their own paragraphs. Editing practice helps students correct common mistakes with the simple present tense. After this, students write the final drafts of their paragraphs.

 EXPLORING WRITTEN ENGLISH
(pages 15–17)

A Noticing

While completing the exercise, students are expected to notice that the simple present tense can be used for both general facts and routines. This exercise is to be done before going over the information in the *Language for Writing* box.

- Have students complete the task individually.
- Check answers as a class. Ask students what all the sentences have in common.

Language for Writing: Review of the Simple Present Tense

The *Language for Writing* box reviews the simple present tense. For both routines and general facts, students should use the simple present tense. Routines include habits and things that happen regularly. General facts are statements that are true, or believed to be true, at the moment.

B Language for Writing

Students practice using the information in the box by underlining the simple present tense verbs in the sentences in exercise **A**.

- Allow students time to complete the activity individually.
- Have them check their answers in pairs.
- Check answers as a class. Ask students: Which sentences are in the third-person singular? What are the subjects of those sentences?

C Language for Writing

Students complete the sentences with the verbs in parentheses. Remind students to notice which sentences are in the third-person singular.

- Allow students time to complete the task individually.
- Check answers as a class. Elicit example sentences from students.

D Language for Writing

Students write three sentences about routines they do that make them happy. Explain that when students apply the strategies to their own lives, it will help them to learn language skills as well. Remind students to use the simple present tense.

- Allow students time to complete the task individually.
- Have students check their answers with a partner.
- Ask volunteers to share their answers with the class.

E Language for Writing

Students write three sentences that describe facts about their country or community. Remind students to use the simple present tense.

- Allow students time to complete the task individually.
- Have students check their answers with a partner.
- Ask volunteers to share their answers with the class.

See Grammar Reference on page 219 of the Student Book for additional information on the simple present tense.

ANSWER KEY

EXPLORING WRITTEN ENGLISH

A **1.** F; **2.** R; **3.** F; **4.** F; **5.** R; **6.** R; **7.** F; **8.** R; **9.** R

LANGUAGE FOR WRITING

B **1.** <u>are</u>
   2. <u>work</u>
   3. <u>offers</u>
   4. <u>live</u>
   5. <u>go</u>
   6. <u>have</u>
   7. <u>is</u>
   8. <u>cycle</u>
   9. <u>reports</u>

C **1.** spend
   2. are; offers
   3. provides; has (Note: *Everyone* and *no one* take the third-person singular.)
   4. don't feel; aren't
   5. have; grow; eat

D Answers will vary. Possible answers:

1. I exercise three times a week.
2. I spend time with my family and friends every weekend.
3. I study English every day.

E Answers will vary. Possible answers:

1. My community includes people of over 15 different nationalities.
2. Our government offers tax breaks to parents of young children.
3. My country is a democracy.

Writing Skill: Writing a Strong Topic Sentence

The *Writing Skill* box explains that main ideas are introduced by topic sentences. A topic sentence is usually the first sentence in a paragraph, but it can appear anywhere in the paragraph. The *Writing Skill* box teaches students the difference between a weak topic sentence, which is too general, and a strong topic sentence, which has enough information for the reader to understand the main idea.

F Writing Skill

Students should refer to the information in the *Writing Skill* box to determine which paragraph has a stronger topic sentence than the others.
- Allow students time to complete the task individually.
- Check answers as a class. Ask why **1** and **3** are not strong topic sentences.

G Writing Skill

Students should refer to the information in the *Writing Skill* box to rewrite the weak topic sentences in exercise **F**.
- Allow time for students to complete the task in pairs. Walk around, and provide assistance as needed.
- Ask volunteers to write their revised topic sentences on the board. Ask students to explain why they chose to make the changes. Discuss these as a class.

 WRITING TASK *(page 18)*

A Brainstorming

Remind students that brainstorming is a useful first step for gathering ideas before writing. Read the *Goal* box aloud so students are familiar with the writing task before brainstorming. Have them list as many reasons as possible why people are happy and unhappy in their community. Students should consider people of all ages and circumstances. Remind students to draw on what they've learned about happiness in this unit.
- Provide one or two example ideas. Ideas should be briefly worded. They need not be listed in any order.
- Allow time for students to complete the task individually.
- Have students share their ideas in pairs and offer feedback to each other.

B Planning

Students choose their three best reasons and write a topic sentence that links them. Point out that each reason is a supporting idea and that students need to add details to each supporting idea. Remind students that complete sentences are not necessary. It is more important to focus on organizing the information.
- Allow time for students to complete their outlines individually. Provide assistance as needed.

C First Draft

Have students write first drafts of their paragraphs based on their outlines.
- Allow time for students to complete the task individually. Provide assistance as needed. Refrain from error correction at this point.

WRITING TASK

A   Answers will vary. Possible answers:

Things people in my community are happy about: safe neighborhoods; green spaces; good schools

Things people in my community are unhappy about: not enough jobs; not enough public transportation; high taxes

B   Answers will vary. Possible answers:

Topic Sentence: People in my community are generally happy.

Reason 1: green spaces

Detail(s): three parks in the middle of the city; people go there to relax, enjoy nature, jog, meet friends, walk their dogs

REVISING PRACTICE *(page 19)*

The *Revising Practice* box contains an exercise that demonstrates several ways students can improve their first drafts.

- Allow time for students to analyze the two drafts and complete the exercise.
- Check answers as a class. Ask students to identify each change and explain how it makes the revised draft stronger.

D Revised Draft

Students should apply the revision techniques used in the *Revising Practice* box to their own drafts, where applicable.

- Explain to students that they will be using the questions as a guide for checking and improving their drafts.
- As a class, go over the questions carefully to make sure students understand them.
- Allow students time to revise their paragraphs.

EDITING PRACTICE *(page 20)*

The *Editing Practice* box trains students to spot and correct common errors related to the use of the simple present tense. As a class, go over the information in the box carefully to make sure students understand what to look out for.

- Allow students time to complete the exercise individually.
- Check answers as a class by asking students to read their corrected sentences aloud and explain the errors.

REVISING PRACTICE

d, a, c, b

EDITING PRACTICE

1. I enjoy the work that I do because it's very challenging, but I <u>don't</u> like my boss.

2. My co-workers are supportive, friendly, and fun, and I <u>enjoy</u> spending time with them after work.

3. It's important to me to spend time with my family members, but it's difficult because they don't <u>live</u> close to me.

4. Although my house is not big and fancy, my neighborhood <u>is</u> very safe.

5. My friends and I <u>exercise</u> together every day to stay healthy, and that contributes to our happiness.

6. My grandfather is still very active and <u>spends</u> a lot of time outdoors. (Note: Here, two verbs, *is* and *spends*, have the same subject—*grandfather*.)

7. Most happy people <u>have</u> hobbies like hiking or playing a musical instrument.

E Final Draft

Have students apply the skills taught in *Editing Practice* to their own revised drafts and check for any other errors.

- Allow time for students to work individually on editing their drafts.
- Walk around, and monitor students as they work. Provide assistance as needed.
- Collect their work once they have completed it.
- For the next class, show anonymous examples of good paragraphs and common errors.

10 MINS UNIT REVIEW

Students can work in groups on this recap of the unit. For question **1**, encourage students to use the target words when appropriate. For questions **2** and **3**, encourage them to check the relevant pages of the unit for answers.

- Allow students time to answer the three questions in groups. For question **1**, ask groups to decide which factors they think are the most important for happiness.
- Ask each group to present its answer for question **1**. Have the class vote for what they believe is the most important factor for happiness.

INVENTIVE SOLUTIONS

2

ACADEMIC TRACK

Technology

ACADEMIC SKILLS

READING	Identifying details
WRITING	Supporting the main idea and giving details
GRAMMAR	Review of the simple past tense
CRITICAL THINKING	Analyzing problems and solutions

UNIT OVERVIEW

The theme of this unit is inventive solutions to problems in developing countries. In two of the inventions described in the unit, windmills in Africa and solar heaters in Egypt, recycled materials are used. The other inventions are also inexpensive and address important humanitarian aid issues. The unit discusses the need for creativity and persistence in problem solving.

- **READING 1:** A young boy in Africa finds a way to help his community by building a windmill out of recycled products.

- **VIDEO:** Using recycled materials in Cairo, one man helps residents build solar heaters to provide hot water to city dwellers.

- **READING 2:** Three inventions for communities in developing countries—an infant warmer, a water container, and a health detector—show that innovations can be inexpensive but have far-reaching effects.

Students draw on what they've read and watched to write a problem-solution paragraph about an innovation. The unit prepares them by introducing vocabulary to talk about inventions and reviewing the simple past tense. It explains the importance of identifying details and the organization of a problem-solution paragraph. Lastly, it reviews brainstorming and outlining techniques.

 THINK AND DISCUSS *(page 21)*

The questions help prepare students for the subject matter covered in the unit— inventions. The scene shows Bundei Hidreka and Rohim Miniaka in rural India. Bundei is teaching Rohim how to make a solar lamp.

- Have students study the picture, title, and caption.
- Discuss the photo as a class. What do students think the photo and the unit are about? Provide your own overview.
- Discuss the two questions as a class. For question **1**, elicit examples from different areas, such as medicine and technology. For question **2**, allow students time to think of as many inventions as possible, and create a word web on the board.

ANSWER KEY

THINK AND DISCUSS

Answers will vary. Possible answers:

1. Alexander Graham Bell; he invented the telephone.

2. train; pencil; chalkboard

EXPLORE THE THEME *(pages 22–23)*

The opening spread provides information and a timeline about inventions throughout history.

- Allow time for students to study the spread and answer the questions individually.
- Check answers as a class. Ask students what inventions surprised them and what inventions they think should have been mentioned.
- Elicit example sentences from students for each of the blue words.

ANSWER KEY

EXPLORE THE THEME

A   Answers will vary. Possible answers:

  1. I agree that these are important inventions. I'd add the lightbulb, the airplane, and the ballpoint pen.

  2. Six of the inventions were developed within the last 200 years (comparatively recently). I think this is because some of them build on each other. For example, the personal computer, the World Wide Web, and the smartphone are connected and all of them need electricity to work.

B   design

    efficient

    equipment

Reading 1

30 MINS

PREPARING TO READ (page 24)

A Building Vocabulary

The sentences are about inventions. They contain seven key vocabulary items that appear in the passage. Students should use contextual clues to deduce the meanings of the words.

- Have students work individually to complete the exercise.
- Check answers as a class. Elicit example sentences. Ask: What is something that you can't afford but would like to have? What is something that you struggle with? What is one way that people try to prevent themselves from getting sick?

See Vocabulary Extension 2A on page 204 of the Student Book for additional practice with Word Partners: adjective + power; power + noun.

B Using Vocabulary

Students should use the new vocabulary items while discussing the two questions.

- Have students work in pairs to discuss the questions.
- Discuss answers as a class. Elicit example answers from students. Compare ways that students are creative. Make a list of sources of electricity on the board.

C Brainstorming

Each idea should be brief. Elicit one or two examples before students begin. Offer one or two examples (television, hair dryer).

- Have students work individually to complete the exercise.
- Have them compare answers in groups of three or four.
- Elicit sample answers from different groups in the class, and create a word web on the board with the answers.

Ideas for... **EXPANSION**

Write these quotes on the board:

I have not failed. I've just found 10,000 ways that won't work.
  – Thomas Edison (1847–1931)

Let me tell you the secret that has led me to my goal. My strength lies solely in my tenacity.
  – Louis Pasteur (1822–1895)

(Note: *solely* = only; *tenacity* = persistence; he didn't give up!)

Ask students what they think these quotes mean. Can they apply to students' lives as well? Have students discuss in pairs and then with the class. Then, if computers are available, have students search online for famous quotes by other inventors and share these findings with the class.

D Predicting

The opening paragraph describes how difficult it is for people in Malawi, Africa, to access electricity. Remind students to skim the first paragraph but also to look at the title, captions, and graphics when predicting what an article is about.

- Allow time for students to skim the first paragraph and look at the title and captions.
- Have students discuss their answers in pairs.
- Discuss as a class. Revisit this question after completing the reading.

ANSWER KEY

PREPARING TO READ

A 1. power
  2. eventually
  3. electricity
  4. prevention
  5. afford
  6. struggle
  7. creative

B Answers will vary. Possible answers:
  1. Yes; baking cakes
  2. sun, wind, nuclear energy, coal, natural gas, water, and thermal

C Answers will vary. Possible answers:
  1. cell phone charger
  2. lights
  3. microwave
  4. ceiling fans
  5. refrigerator
  6. alarm clock

D b (Note: Based on the first paragraph, the answer could be option a, but after looking at the pictures and captions, the correct answer is option b.)

🎧 1.03 Have students read the passage individually, or play the audio and have students read along.

OVERVIEW OF THE READING

The passage is about how William Kamkwamba, a 14-year-old boy, built a windmill in his village in Malawi, Africa. Using an instruction book from the library and recycled material, Kamkwamba built his first windmill and then additional windmills to provide electricity for his village. He continues to educate and provide solutions to his community.

Online search terms: William Kamkwamba TED Talk; Moving Windmills Project; BBC Malawi Windmill

UNDERSTANDING THE READING
(page 27)

A Understanding the Main Idea

Students are asked to choose the best alternative title for the reading passage.

- Have students complete the activity individually.
- Check answers as a class. Ask students why they chose this title.

B Understanding Details

Students test their understanding of the details in the passage by answering the questions.

- Allow students time to write their answers individually.
- Have them check their answers in pairs.

C Critical Thinking: Analyzing Problems and Solutions

The *Critical Thinking* box explains how to analyze problems and solutions. In a reading, the problem is usually stated first, followed by solutions. In this exercise, students should read the chart and write solutions below the problems. Encourage students to review the reading passage to fill in the chart. Complete the first solution with the class as an example.

- Allow time for students to complete the task in pairs.
- Check answers as a class. Write the chart on the board, and elicit example answers.

Ideas for… EXPANSION

To supplement Exercise C, have students work in groups of three or four to create a dialogue about the story. They should first discuss what William's family and the people in the village said to him when he wanted to build a windmill. What was his response? Have students write, practice, and present the dialogue to the class.

D Critical Thinking: Analyzing

Students should review the chart in exercise C and then discuss alternative solutions.

- Have students write ideas individually.
- Have them discuss their solutions in pairs.
- Discuss as a class.

UNDERSTANDING THE READING

A   c (Note: Although the article has advice for inventors and is about windmills, the main idea is that William brought electricity to his community.)

B   Wording of answers will vary. Correct answers:

1. There was a drought. (Paragraph B)
2. People laughed at his idea and didn't believe he could do it. (Paragraph D)
3. People used it to get power for their cell phones. (Paragraph E)

C   Wording of answers will vary. Correct answers:

Problems:

He couldn't buy the equipment he needed. (Paragraph D)

Solutions (from left to right):

He went to the library. (Paragraph C)

He looked at the pictures in the book. (Paragraph C)

William built a second windmill to bring water up from underground. (Paragraph E)

William taught other people how to build windmills and created a website. (Paragraphs E and F)

D   Answers will vary. Possible answer: He could have looked for a part-time job to earn some money for school fees.

DEVELOPING READING SKILLS *(page 28)*

Reading Skill: Identifying Details

The *Reading Skill* box explains how to identify supporting ideas. Supporting ideas help to explain the main idea by giving reasons and examples. By framing the main idea with *wh-* question words, students can identify the information that the supporting details provide. On the board, draw a diagram that looks like a funnel. Write *Topic*, *Main Idea*, and then *Supporting Ideas* in descending order in the diagram. Remind students that the supporting ideas are more specific than the main idea, which is more specific than the topic. Elicit another example topic (school), the main idea (This is the best class), and the supporting ideas (The students are very friendly).

A Identifying the Main Idea and Details

Students should read the paragraph and find the main idea and the three supporting details.

- Allow time for students to complete the task individually.
- Have students compare their answers in pairs.
- Check answers as a class. Ask students to use *wh-* questions to explain how they arrived at their answers: *What* did he invent? *Why* did he invent it? *How* does it work?

B Identifying Details

Have students locate two supporting details in the reading passage to find one that gives a reason and one that gives an example. Encourage students to review the explanation in the *Reading Skills* box for clarification. Point out that there will be more than one example of each in the reading passage.

- Allow students time to complete the task individually.
- Have them compare their answers in pairs.
- Discuss answers as a class. As volunteers read their sentences, have the class decide whether they are *reasons* or *examples*.

Video

⏱ **VIEWING: SOLAR SOLUTIONS** *(pages 29–30)*

Overview of the Video

The video tells the story of Thomas Taha Culhane and his solar heater project on Cairo's rooftops. Because trash and recycled materials are used, these solar water heaters are inexpensive to make. Because of Cairo's heat, solar panels absorb heat and provide hot water to people in the city. This, in turn, cuts down on energy costs and uses renewable energy.

Online search terms: Thomas Taha Culhane National Geographic; Solar Cities

BEFORE VIEWING

A Predicting

Students should think of reasons for using solar power.

- Have students to study the photo, title, and caption.
- Have students discuss their ideas with a partner.
- Discuss as a class. Ask students whether anyone has used solar power before. What are some pros and cons?

B Learning About the Topic

The paragraph prepares students for the video by giving them background information about solar technology, which is further explained in the video.

- Have students complete the task individually.
- Check answers as a class.

C Vocabulary in Context

This exercise introduces students to some of the key words used in the video. The sentences are quotes from the video that provide information about the topic. Point out that the answers use the words in their base forms (*going green = go green*).

- Have students complete the task individually.
- Check answers as a class. Elicit sample sentences for each word. Ask: What are some ways that your community is *going green*? Are you an *urban dweller*? What's one way to *cut down on* the amount of trash you create? What's a *no-brainer* when it comes to the environment?

BEFORE VIEWING

A Answers will vary. Possible answers:

It's good for the environment, and it won't run out.

B 1. There is a lot of it (*enough to fulfill all the world's power needs many times over*).

2. Answers will vary. Possible answers: solar hot water panels and solar electric panels; solar hot water panels, because they are cheaper and easier to make.

C 1. cut down on

2. go green

3. no-brainer

4. dweller

WHILE VIEWING

A ▶ Understanding Main Ideas

Have students read the items silently before you play the video. Tell students that there are two goals, so they will check more than one option.

• Have them complete the task while the video is playing.

• Check answers as a class. Discuss why the other statements are incorrect.

B ▶ Understanding Details

Have students read the questions and write any answers they recall from the first viewing before playing the video a second time.

• Have students complete the task while the video is playing.

• Check answers as a class. Have volunteers share their answers. Ask whether there was anything that surprised them in the video.

WHILE VIEWING

A 1, 3

B Answers will vary. Possible answers:

1. local community materials, recycled materials, and some garbage

2. Cairo gets a lot of sunshine.

3. Dust from the nearby desert gets on the panels. A simple solution is to wipe the dust away. (Note: *Dust* is the term for small particles of earth and other materials that form a powder.)

AFTER VIEWING

A Reacting to the Video

Students are asked to reflect on the information in the video and relate it to their own lives.

• Allow students time to discuss the questions in pairs.

• Discuss as a class. For question **2**, show the last scene in the video again, and then discuss the quote.

B Critical Thinking: Synthesizing

Students draw on information from both Reading 1 and the Video to synthesize their answers. Ask students to skim through Reading 1 again to refresh their memories.

• Allow students time to discuss their answers pairs.

• Discuss as a class. Elicit example answers from students, and write them on the board.

Ideas for… EXPANSION

Have students tell personal stories about an innovation that they remember from growing up. Example: *We didn't have a swing so we tied rope to a tree. It didn't work because the tree branch fell down!*

1) What did they need to do?

2) How did they (or someone else in their community) try to achieve this?

3) Did it work? Why or why not?

Allow students time to write down ideas. Then have students tell their stories in groups of three or four. Have the other members of the group ask *wh-*questions to learn more about the story. (Examples: *Who* was with you? *Where* did this happen?). Have each group choose the most interesting story to share with the class.

AFTER VIEWING

A 1. Answers will vary. Possible answer: Yes, they would work well in my country because we have hot weather and sunshine all year round.

2. garbage; treasure. This saying means that some people can use things that other people think are worthless.

B Answers will vary. Possible answers:

Both inventions use renewable energy; they are inexpensive; they are made from recycled materials; the community had to be convinced that the invention would work.

Reading 2

PREPARING TO READ (page 31)

A Building Vocabulary

In this exercise, the definitions of eight key words from the reading passage are provided. Students should use the definitions to help them complete the exercise. Remind students to use the correct forms of the words.

- Have students complete the task individually.
- Check answers as a class. Elicit example sentences for each vocabulary item. Ask: What's a container you use every day? What is something that is very valuable to you? What is one way that you can indicate agreement without speaking? What is a benefit of learning English?

See Vocabulary Extension 2B on page 204 of the Student Book for additional practice with Word Link: -able and -ible.

B Using Vocabulary

Students should use the new vocabulary items while discussing the two questions.

- Have students work in pairs to answer the questions. Give students one or two examples of innovations and devices.
- Check answers as a class. Elicit example answers from students.

C Predicting

Students should skim through the first paragraph and read the title and subheads to make their own guesses about this reading. Stress that students should not try to read the entire passage. You may want to time the students by giving them one minute to skim the material.

- Have students skim through the first paragraph, photos, and subheads.
- Have students discuss the passage in pairs.
- Discuss answers as a class. Write the following subheads on the board: *Infant Warmer, Water Container,* and *Health Detector*. Write students' ideas in word webs next to each of the items. Allow students to write down predictions, and explain that they will revisit their predictions later to see whether they were correct.

🎧 1.04   Have students read the passage individually, or play the audio and have students read along.

OVERVIEW OF THE READING

The reading passage describes three inventions for developing countries. All three—an infant warmer, a water container, and a health detector—are inexpensive and have far-reaching effects.

Online search terms: *Jane Chen TED Talk; Q drum; Hayat Sindi National Geographic*

A Understanding Main Ideas

Students read the chart and choose the sentence that summarizes the purpose of each product. Elicit the meanings of *regulate* (control), *remote* (far away from others), and *accurately* (correctly).

- Have students complete the task individually.
- Check answers as a class. Ask students where they found their answers.

B Identifying Details

Students are asked to find supporting details mentioned in the passage. Ask whether they were correct in their earlier predictions about the three items.

- Allow time for students to complete the task individually.
- Have students check their answers in pairs.
- Check answers as a class.

C Critical Thinking: Evaluating

Students should identify what makes an innovation useful and reflect on the items from both the video and the reading. Encourage students to review the reading and their notes on the video again.

- Allow students time to answer the questions individually.
- Have them discuss their answers in groups of three or four and give reasons to justify their choices. Encourage students to try to convince their group to agree with them.
- Discuss as a class. As a class, vote for the best invention.

Ideas for… EXPANSION

Four Corners: Designate each corner of the room for a different invention, with a piece of paper placed on the wall naming this invention. (Note: You can use the inventions listed in exercise C or, if students have already done the exercise, you can use four other inventions instead.)

1. Give students 30 seconds to choose the invention they think is best and ask them to stand in that corner.

2. Have students discuss in their groups why they chose that corner. They should write brief ideas on the paper.

3. Tell students that an investor will donate money to the invention that wins the Best Invention award. If possible, show a clip from the show *Shark Tank*. Allow time for the groups to create a list of reasons, using their earlier notes, to convince the investor to choose their invention.

4. Ask each group to present their reasons to the class and encourage other students to ask questions.

5. Students vote for the best invention.(You may want to tell them they need to vote for an invention other than their own.)

ANSWER KEY

UNDERSTANDING THE READING

A   Embrace Infant Warmer: a (See Paragraph C.)

Q Drum: b (See Paragraph E.)

Health Detector: a (See Paragraph G.)

B 1. less than 5.5 pounds (2.5 kilograms)

2. People in developing countries usually have to carry heavy containers of water on their heads.

3. paper; it's light and easy to carry, so health workers can easily bring it with them to perform tests in patients' homes.

4. Answers will vary. Possible answers:

They are inexpensive; they help people in developing countries; they are easy to use; they can work without electricity.

C   Answers will vary. Possible answer:

I'd choose the solar-powered water heater, because it's very easy to make, it will help keep many people healthy and warm, and it's good for the environment.

Writing

OVERVIEW

In this section, students progress from focusing on topic sentences in the previous unit to focusing on identifying supporting ideas in order to write a problem-solution paragraph. The lesson starts by reviewing the simple past tense and then teaches students about supporting details. In the *Writing Task*, students apply these lessons by writing a paragraph about an important innovation. As added support, they will encounter two drafts of a sample paragraph. Students begin the task by brainstorming for ideas and reasons before selecting the best ones and organizing them in an outline. Students then draft their paragraphs, improve their drafts, and correct common mistakes that occur when ideas are connected.

 EXPLORING WRITTEN ENGLISH
(pages 35–37)

A Noticing

While completing the exercise, students are expected to notice that the simple past tense can be used for events that began and ended in the past. This exercise is to be done before going over the information in the *Language for Writing* box. Point out that the sentences are all excerpts from Readings **1** and **2**.
• Have students complete the task individually.
• Check answers as a class. Ask students what sentences **3** and **4** have in common.

Language for Writing: Review of the Simple Past Tense

The *Language for Writing* box provides examples of use of the simple past tense. In Unit 1, students reviewed the simple present tense for facts and routines. In this unit, they review using the simple past tense to talk about events that began and ended in the past. Highlight how the simple past tense is formed differently for *be* and other verbs. Note that forms of *be* (*was/were*) change depending on the subject, but other verbs stay the same for all subjects. Review the formation for the affirmative and negative. Remind students that past tense forms of irregular verbs need to be memorized.

B Language for Writing

Students complete the sentences using the simple past tense of the verbs in the parentheses. Refer students to the *Language for Writing* box for help with the simple past verb formation and for a list of irregular verbs. If

computers are available, encourage students to study irregular verbs online, on websites such as Quizlet.
• Allow students time to complete the activity individually.
• Have them check answers in pairs.
• Check answers as a class. Ask students which verbs are irregular, and make a list on the board.

C Language for Writing

Students write four sentences about how people did things in the past. Explain that they can base their ideas on the inventions in this unit or their own ideas. Remind students to use the simple past tense.
• Allow students time to complete the task individually.
• Have students check their answers with a partner.
• Ask volunteers to share their answers with the class.

> **Ideas for EXPANSION**
>
> Have students use the irregular verbs found in exercises A and B to write three true sentences and one false sentence about themselves. Have students read their sentences aloud in small groups. Their group should guess which sentence is false.

See Grammar Reference on page 220 of the Student Book for additional information on the simple past tense.

ANSWER KEY

EXPLORING WRITTEN ENGLISH

A 1. was; became
   2. didn't know; wasn't; was
   3. changed; improved
   4. invented
   5. came

LANGUAGE FOR WRITING

B 1. was
   2. built; didn't believe
   3. taught
   4. invented; created; allowed
   5. made; gave

C   Answers will vary. Possible answers:
   1. Before the invention of the motor car, people traveled by horse and carriage.
   2. Before the invention of the telephone, people wrote more letters.
   3. Before the invention of the smartphone, people socialized with their friends more in person.
   4. Before the invention of the freezer, people didn't store ice cream in their homes.

Writing Skill: Supporting the Main idea and Giving Details

The *Writing Skill* box explains the importance of supporting the main idea and giving details. The *Writing Skill* box teaches students how to write strong supporting idea sentences by answering <u>wh-</u> questions, repeating key words from the main idea, using transition words, and adding details. It explains the importance of details (descriptions, reasons, facts, and examples) because they help readers understand the passage more clearly.

D Writing Skill

Students should refer to the information in the *Writing Skill* box to identify which sentences provide supporting ideas and which sentences provide details. Have a student read the topic sentence aloud. Elicit how many supporting ideas students should expect to find (three).

• Allow students time to complete the task individually.
• Check answers as a class. Ask students why they chose their answers.

E Writing Skill

Students use the sentences in exercise D to write a paragraph about solar lanterns. Point out that the transition words and phrases are included in the supporting idea sentences and will help them plan their paragraphs. They do not need to write their own ideas.

• Allow time for students to complete the task individually.
• Have students compare their paragraphs in pairs.
• Ask volunteers to share their answers. If possible, write the final version of the paragraph on the board.

ANSWER KEY

WRITING SKILL

D   **1.** D; **2.** D; **3.** SI; **4.** SI; **5.** D; **6.** SI

E   3, 1, 6, 2, 4, 5

Solar lanterns are better than kerosene lamps for bringing light to people in developing countries for three main reasons. First of all, solar-powered lanterns are more efficient than kerosene lamps. For example, they produce 50 times more light than kerosene lamps. Another benefit of solar-powered lanterns is that they are good for the environment. They use solar energy, which is a renewable source of power. Finally, solar lanterns are better for our health. The smoke from kerosene lamps can cause lung damage, but solar-powered lanterns don't use any dangerous chemicals.

WRITING TASK *(page 38)*

A Brainstorming

Remind students that brainstorming is a useful first step for gathering ideas before writing. Read the *Goal* box aloud so students are familiar with the writing task before brainstorming. Have them list as many inventions as they can remember.

• Provide one or two examples (smartphone, the printing press)
• Have students complete the task individually. Give a time limit so that students are motivated to add to their lists quickly.
• Compare answers as a class. Make a list of the inventions on the board.

B Planning

Students choose an invention that they want to write about. Remind students that complete sentences are not necessary. It is more important to focus on organizing their information. Remind students of the difference between the topic sentence, the supporting ideas, and the details. Refer them to the *Writing Skill* box on pages 36 and 37, *Supporting the Main Idea and Giving Details*, for more information.

• Allow time for students to complete their outlines individually. Provide assistance as needed.

C First Draft

Have students write first drafts of their paragraphs based on their outlines.

• Allow time for students to complete the task individually. Provide assistance as needed. Refrain from error correction at this point.

WRITING TASK

A Answers will vary. Possible answers:

ballpoint pens; washing machines; dishwashers; the wheel; the printing press

B Answers will vary. Possible answers:

Topic Sentence: Antibiotics dramatically changed human health.

Supporting Idea 1: In the past, many people died from infections—now cured by antibiotics.

Detail(s): Illnesses such as strep throat or bronchitis – often deadly.

Supporting Idea 2: Even if people didn't die from illnesses, it took them much longer to recover.

Detail(s): Children often missed months of school. With antibiotics, they usually return to school after 24 hours.

REVISING PRACTICE

c, d, a, b

EDITING PRACTICE

1. William Kamkwamba <u>built</u> a windmill using parts he found in junkyards.
2. The people in William Kamkwamba's village <u>weren't</u> confident about his plan.
3. Before Nils Bohlin's invention, most cars <u>had</u> seat belts that were buckled across the stomach.
4. The first car didn't <u>go</u> very fast.
5. Orville Wright <u>made</u> the first powered airplane flight in 1903.
6. Alexander Graham Bell, inventor of the telephone, <u>started</u> the Bell Telephone Company in 1877.
7. Ts'ai Lun invented paper in the first century A.D., but it <u>wasn't</u> widely available until many years later. (Note: "… but it didn't become widely available …" is also correct.)

REVISING PRACTICE (page 39)

The *Revising Practice* box contains an exercise that demonstrates several ways students can improve their first drafts.

- Allow time for students to analyze the two drafts and complete the exercise. Point out that one of the types of changes (*a-d*) can be used more than once.
- Check answers as a class. Ask students to identify each change and explain how it makes the revised draft stronger.

D Revised Draft

Students should apply the revision techniques used in the *Revising Practice* box to their own drafts, where applicable.

- Explain to students that they will be using the questions as a guide for checking and improving their drafts.
- As a class, go over the questions carefully to make sure students understand them.
- Allow students time to revise their paragraphs.

EDITING PRACTICE (page 40)

The *Editing Practice* box trains students to spot and correct common errors related to the use of the simple past tense. As a class, go over the information in the box carefully to make sure students understand what to look out for.

- Allow students time to complete the exercise individually.
- Check answers as a class by asking students to read their corrected sentences aloud and explain the errors.

E Final Draft

Have students apply the skills taught in *Editing Practice* to their own revised drafts and check for any other errors.

- Allow time for students to work individually on editing their drafts.
- Walk around, and monitor students as they work. Provide assistance as needed.
- Collect their work once they have completed it.
- For the next class, show anonymous examples of good paragraphs and common errors.

UNIT REVIEW

Students can work in groups on this recap of the unit. For question **1**, encourage students to use the target words when appropriate. For questions **2** and **3**, encourage them to check the relevant pages of the unit for answers.

- Allow students time to answer the two questions in groups. For question **1**, ask groups to decide which invention they think is the most important.
- Ask each group to present its answer for question **1**. Have students vote for what they believe is the most important invention in history.

CONNECTED LIVES

ACADEMIC TRACK

Communications/Sociology

ACADEMIC SKILLS

READING	Taking notes (Part 1)
WRITING	Writing a concluding sentence
GRAMMAR	Using the present perfect tense
CRITICAL THINKING	Making inferences

UNIT OVERVIEW

The theme of this unit is online communication. It gives examples of ways that people have used the Internet to collaborate with other people around the world.

- **READING 1:** This reading describes two collaborative projects that use crowdsourcing to recruit volunteers to help with work on archaeological sites.

- **VIDEO:** The video shows how Albert Lin's project uses citizen scientists to help search for Genghis Khan's tomb.

- **READING 2:** This reading describes the process that two men started to connect an island in Fiji that needed funds with a larger Internet community of volunteers.

Students draw on what they've read and watched to write a paragraph about a crowdsourcing website. The unit prepares them by introducing vocabulary to talk about online communication, taking notes, and using the present perfect tense. They also learn how to write a concluding sentence. Lastly, students brainstorm to help them plan their paragraphs, and then revise and edit their drafts.

 THINK AND DISCUSS *(page 41)*

The questions help prepare students for the subject matter covered in the unit—online communication. The scene depicts people playing in an online gaming festival in Germany.

- Have students study the picture, title, and captions.
- Discuss the photo as a class. What do students think the unit is about? Provide your own overview.
- Discuss the two questions as a class. For question **1**, create a word web on the board that lists different activities student do online. For question **2**, create a chart that lists ways that our lives have been improved by online communication, and ways they have not.

Ask students if they think online communication has resulted in an overall improvement in our lives.

ANSWER KEY

THINK AND DISCUSS

Answers will vary. Possible answers:

1. email; use social media; research travel destinations; shop; do homework

2. **Yes:** We can communicate with people around the world; we can work any time, any place; we can search quickly for information. **No:** There is less face-to-face communication; people don't "unplug" (have time off from electronics); people rely on the Internet for information instead of thinking for themselves.

 EXPLORE THE THEME *(pages 42–43)*

The opening spread features information about the world's top 10 websites. Draw students' attention to the footnoted terms.

- Allow students time to study the spread and answer the questions in part **A** individually.
- Have students discuss their answers in pairs.
- Discuss answers as a class. For question **1**, ask why they think search engines might be more popular. For question **2**, write a list of websites on the board.
- Have students answer the question in part **B**. Remind students to use the correct forms of the words.
- Elicit example sentences from students for each of the blue words. Elicit other words related to the Internet, and write these on the board.

ANSWER KEY

EXPLORE THE THEME

A 1. Google, YouTube, Facebook; Google, a search engine, is the most popular.

 2. Answers will vary. Possible answers: Google, Facebook; other popular websites: Snapchat, Instagram, Buzzfeed, Weibo

B search; launch; log in

Reading 1

PREPARING TO READ *(page 44)*

A Building Vocabulary

Students find the seven blue words in the passage and use contextual clues to guess the meanings of the words.

- Allow time for students to complete the exercise individually.
- Check answers as a class. Ask which words students already knew. Which ones are new to them? Ask whether students know other forms of the vocabulary words. Note that many of the vocabulary words on this list have noun forms that end in –tion: *participation, investigation, collaboration, and contribution.*
- Elicit example sentences for each vocabulary item. Ask: Is it important to be an active *participant* in English class? Why or why not? What are some *features* of this textbook? Do you like collaborating with others on projects? Why or why not?

See Vocabulary Extension 3A on page 205 of the Student Book for additional practice with Word Partners: adjective + contribution.

B Using Vocabulary

Students should practice using the new vocabulary items while answering the three questions.

- Have students discuss their answers in pairs.
- Compare answers as a class. Elicit example answers from students. For question **1**, ask students what they need to do if they forget their *log in* information. For question **2**, ask if the Internet has *contributed* to their language learning. If so, how?

C Brainstorming

Students create a list of reasons why people use the Internet. Encourage students to use the vocabulary words from exercise A, if possible. Ideas can be brief.

- Have students work in pairs to create a list.
- Discuss the question as a class. On the board, write a list of ideas. Ask students which ideas they think are the most important.

D Predicting

Students look at the title and subheads, and then read the first paragraph of the reading passage. They should decide which answer best describes what the paragraph is about.

- Allow time for students to skim the reading and answer the question. You may want to give a time limit of 1 to 2 minutes.
- Have students check answers in pairs.
- Have students compare their answers with those of other students in the class. Ask them how they arrived at their answers. Revisit this question after the reading.

ANSWER KEY

PREPARING TO READ

A **1.** participant (Note: A *participant* is a person. The action is *participation*.)
   2. investigate
   3. Accurate (Note: A synonym for *accurate* is *precise*.)
   4. collaborate
   5. contribution
   6. potential
   7. feature

B Answers will vary. Possible answers:
   1. I log in to social media sites at least once a day. My favorite sites are Facebook and Instagram.
   2. Social media helps connect people all over the world. During disasters, social media provides access to relevant and timely information. For example, weather agencies used Twitter to post frequent updates on the path of Hurricane Irma as it approached Florida. After the storm, Florida residents used Facebook and Twitter to reassure family and friends that they were safe.

C Answers will vary. Possible answers: to do group projects for school; to start or join an online petition; to raise money for a project (crowdfunding)

D b (Explanation: Option a is untrue because not everyone involved is an archaeologist. Option c is too specific to be the main idea.)

🎧 **1.05** Have students read the passage individually, or play the audio and have students read along.

OVERVIEW OF THE READING

The reading passage describes two crowdsourcing projects, both related to archaeology. Lin's project focuses on finding the tomb of Genghis Khan. Parcak hopes to find and preserve archaeological sites in Peru, protecting them from looting and illegal construction.

Online search terms: Genghis Khan; Albert Lin; Sarah Parcak; GlobalXplorer

UNDERSTANDING THE READING *(page 47)*

A Understanding the Main Idea

Students choose the correct statement to explain crowdsourcing. Elicit the meaning of *enabling* (making something possible).

- Have students complete the activity individually.
- Check answer as a class. Ask students how *crowdsourcing* might have received this name. (What is a crowd? What is a source?)

B Identifying Details

Students test their understanding of the details in the passage by completing a chart.

- Allow students time to complete the chart individually.
- Have them form pairs and compare their answers.
- Check answers as a class. Ask where they found the information to arrive at their answers. Elicit that *an unmarked grave* means we don't know where it was. A *tile* is usually a small square used in construction. Ask students why they think these areas of land are called *tiles*.

C Critical Thinking: Making Inferences

The *Critical Thinking* box describes the importance of making guesses when reading. Elicit the meaning of "read between the lines" by drawing three lines on the board. Scribble on the top and bottom line and point to the middle line. Explain that there aren't any words here, but there is space for a reader to think about the meaning of the passage. Have a student read the text in the box aloud. You may want to discuss the first example as a class.

- Have students answer the questions individually.
- Have students check answers in pairs.
- Discuss the answers as a class. Ask students how they arrived at their answers.

D Critical Thinking: Reflecting

Have students think about what they have read and discuss their personal opinions. Remind them to justify their opinions.

- Have students discuss their answers in pairs.
- Discuss answers as a class. Take a vote to see who would like to join each project. If students wouldn't like to join either project, have them explain their reasons.

Ideas for… EXPANSION

Ask students to imagine that they have been asked by Lin or Parcak to create a webpage about one of the two projects to attract more volunteers. Have them work in groups of three or four. What information would they put on the page? What images would they use? Have them sketch the webpage and show the class. Then have them search online for the webpages about each project. Are they similar to or different from their ideas? Why do they think this is?

ANSWER KEY

UNDERSTANDING THE READING

A   b

B 1. Mongolia (See Paragraphs B and C.)
   2. Genghis Khan (See Paragraphs B.)
   3. unusual (See Paragraph D.)
   4. Peru (See Paragraph F.)
   5. looters (See Paragraph F.)
   6. illegal construction (See Paragraph F.)

C 1. b; 2. b; 3. a

D   Answers will vary. Possible answers: I'd prefer to join Lin's project because I'm fascinated by Genghis Khan. OR I'd prefer to join Parcak's project because I would like to help protect these important sites from looters.

DEVELOPING READING SKILLS *(page 48)*

Reading Skill: Taking Notes (Part 1)

The *Reading Skill* box explains two benefits of taking notes: understanding and organizing the information. Have volunteers read the text in the box and the examples aloud. Ask students which of the types of graphic organizers they like best. Are there any that they haven't tried yet?

A Understanding a Process

Have students read the paragraph about Parcak's project and underline the steps in the process. Encourage students to number each step. You may want to offer one example to start.

- Allow time for students to complete the task individually.
- Have students check answers in pairs.

B Taking Notes

Students complete the flow chart using the information in exercise **A**. Elicit the meaning of a flow chart. (It shows how one thing leads to another in a process.)

- Have students complete the flow chart individually.
- Have students check their answers in pairs.
- Check answers as a class. Ask students whether they find it easier to read the information in a flow chart than in paragraph form.

Ideas for… EXPANSION

Have students think about a process that they know well, such as making an omelet or changing a tire. Have them work in pairs to create a flow chart with at least six steps. Tell them not to give the flow chart a title. Then have the other students read the flow charts and guess what process is being described. Afterward, ask whether students think that writing the flow chart helped them speak about the process clearly.

ANSWER KEY

DEVELOPING READING SKILLS

A Participants first watch online videos that teach them how to identify certain features on satellite images.

Then they study and flag satellite images on their own.

Once enough volunteers say that they see the same thing, …

… Parcak and her team will check for themselves …

… before passing the information along to archaeologists on the ground.

The "players" receive a score based on how accurate they are.

B **1.** online videos

2. flag

3. see the same thing

4. check

5. archaeologists

6. accurate

Video

40 MINS **VIEWING: CITIZEN SCIENTISTS**
(pages 49-50)

Overview of the Video

The video shows how Albert Lin's project uses citizen scientists from around the world to search for Genghis Khan's tomb. Although the citizen scientists did not find his tomb, the video shows one ancient tomb found through their crowdsourcing.

Online search terms: Albert Lin Mongolia; Genghis Khan tomb; Mongolia; Burkhan Khaldun

BEFORE VIEWING

A Brainstorming

Have students look at the picture and read the caption. What adjectives would they use to describe Mongolia? Then ask them what they know about Genghis Khan. What would they like to learn about him?

- Have students discuss possible reasons in pairs.
- Discuss answers with the class. Write ideas on the board, and revisit this question after watching the video to see if students' predictions were correct.

B Learning about the Topic

The paragraph prepares students for the video by giving them background information about Genghis Khan. Have students read the paragraph and answer the questions.

- Have students complete the task individually.
- Have students check answers in pairs.
- Check answers as a class. If a map of the area that the Mongol Empire covered is available, show it to the class.

C Vocabulary in Context

This exercise introduces students to some of the key words used in the video. Encourage students to try to infer the meanings from the context. Remind students to use the correct word form for each word.

- Have students complete the task individually.
- Check answers as a class. Elicit example sentences for each word. Ask: Why might someone *tag* an animal in the wild? Do you think English phrases are difficult to *figure out*? Why or why not? How long will you wait for something to *upload* before you get annoyed?

ANSWER KEY

BEFORE VIEWING

A Answers will vary. Possible answers: because they want to help solve the mystery and be part of history; because Genghis Khan was a powerful leader

B Answers will vary. Possible answers:

1. because he launched violent military campaigns against his enemies

2. a. He devised a system of laws and regulations.

   b. He allowed freedom of religion.

C 1. tag

2. figure out

3. upload

WHILE VIEWING

A ▶ Understanding the Main Idea

Have students read the items silently before you play the video. Then have the students watch the video and choose the best title from the list of options. Have them complete the task while the video is playing.

• Have students form pairs and compare answers.

• Check answers as a class.

B ▶ Understanding Details

Have students fill in any answers that they recall from the first viewing before playing the video a second time. Elicit the meanings of *traces*, *satellites*, and *check it out*.

• Have students complete the task while the video is playing.

• Have students form pairs and compare answers.

• Check answers as a class. Ask if there are any other words that they need to have explained, and elicit definitions from volunteers.

ANSWER KEY

WHILE VIEWING

A a (Note: This option provides the most complete answer.)

B Answers will vary. Possible answers:

1. straight lines

2. It's too old.

3. Because if citizen scientists can find this tomb, they can probably find other tombs, too.

AFTER VIEWING

A Reacting to the Video

Students should use the information they learned from the video and Reading 1 to discuss the question.

• Have students discuss their answers in pairs.

• Discuss as a class. Have students share the questions they would ask Lin. Write these on the board.

B Critical Thinking: Analyzing

Students read a quote from Reading 1 and connect this to the information in the video.

• Allow students time to answer the question individually.

• Have students discuss their answers in pairs.

• Discuss as a class. Ask students whether they think *they* would be good citizen scientists? Why or why not?

ANSWER KEY

AFTER VIEWING

A Answers will vary. Possible answers: Why do you want to find the tomb? What were some challenges you faced in Mongolia? What do Mongolians think about this project? What would you say to Genghis Khan if you could meet him?

B Answers will vary. Possible answer: I think Lin means that computers can't make inferences or notice when things don't look natural, as people can. In the video, he says that straight lines usually indicate that something is man-made, and he mentions that many citizen scientists tagged an unusual rectangle shape on the satellite map.

Ideas for… EXPANSION

Have students do more research on Genghis Khan. First, have them make a KWL chart. This chart has three columns: what I know, what I want to know, and what I learned. Have them fill out the first two columns in pairs. Then they should research Genghis Khan and fill in the third column. Have them discuss with their partner what they learned, and then compare their chart with a chart created by another pair of students. Ask volunteers to share what information they found most interesting.

Reading 2

PREPARING TO READ (page 51)

A Building Vocabulary

In this exercise, students read the definitions of the eight vocabulary words from the reading passage. Then they choose the correct word for each sentence.

- Have students complete the exercise individually.
- Check answers as a class. Elicit example sentences for each vocabulary item. Ask: What kind of *advertisements* do you think are the most effective? What are some *tools* you use for learning English? Do you feel as if you belong to a *global* community? Why or why not?

See Vocabulary Extension 3B on page 205 of the Student Book for additional practice with Word Link: -al.

B Using Vocabulary

Students should use the new vocabulary items while discussing the two questions.

- Have students work in pairs to answer the questions.
- Discuss answers as a class. Elicit example answers from students. Ask students to give examples of *virtual* communication pros and cons in their own life. Ask students to describe the *remote* place they mentioned.

C Predicting

Remind students to skim the first paragraph and to look at the title and subheads when predicting what an article is about.

- Allow time for students to skim the reading and look at the title and subheads. Set a time limit of 1 to 2 minutes.
- Have students discuss their answers in pairs.
- Discuss as a class. Have students read the subheads aloud to see whether that can help them with their predictions. Revisit this question after completing the reading.

1.06 Have students read the passage individually, or play the audio and have students read along.

OVERVIEW OF THE READING

The reading passage tells the story of Tribewanted.com. Using social media, the founders, Keene and James, began their first project—on a small island in Fiji—by gathering a group of people who wanted to help develop sustainable projects together with the local community. Keene and James have gone on to found other tribes in Papua New Guinea, Bali, Italy, and more.

Online search terms: Tribewanted; Ben Keene; Vorovoro

UNDERSTANDING THE READING *(page 54)*

A Understanding Main Ideas

Students read the passage and then choose three of the five sentences provided to complete a summary of the passage. Elicit the meaning of *sharing music* (uploading and downloading music files online) and *newcomers* (people who have arrived somewhere for the first time). Ask students whether their predictions about the passage were accurate.

• Allow time for students to complete the task individually.

• Check answers as a class. Ask students how they arrived at their answers.

B Identifying Details

Students read the statements and complete the sentences with information from the reading. Point out that the information does not appear in the same order as it does in the reading passage.

• Allow time for students to complete the task individually.

• Have students check answers in pairs.

• Check answers as a class.

C Sequencing

Students complete the timeline with the information from exercise B. Elicit that the box on the far left (with "5") happened first. The box on the far right happened most recently. You may also want to explain that it doesn't matter that the boxes are above or below the line; this is just a way to fit more information in a smaller space.

• Allow students time to complete the timeline individually.

• Have students check answers in pairs.

• Check answers with the class.

D Critical Thinking: Making Inferences

Students discuss the questions, based on the material in the reading passage and their own ideas.

• Have students discuss the questions in pairs.

• Discuss as a class. Ask whether any students want to join Tribewanted. Ask whether anyone has had an experience of meeting people who live a very traditional lifestyle.

ANSWER KEY

UNDERSTANDING THE READING

A a, b, e

B 1. Vorovoro (See paragraph C.)

2. 2006 (See paragraph E.)

3. $53,000 (See paragraph D.)

4. Tribewanted.com (See paragraph C.)

5. email (See paragraph A.)

6. Bali (See paragraph H.)

7. local (See paragraph F.)

C From left to right: 5, 4, 1, 3, 2, 7, 6

D Answers will vary. Possible answers:

1. I think the people who join Tribewanted are adventurous and like to travel. They want to help protect the environment and make a positive contribution to other people's lives. They are likely to be more interested in work that they enjoy doing and find fulfilling, and are less motivated by money. They also probably like being around a diverse group of people.

2. I think Tui Mali and his tribe members have become more aware of different cultures and feel more connected with the rest of the world now. Although their island has become more modern, they probably still maintain some important aspects of their traditional culture. (See paragraphs F and G.)

Ideas for... EXPANSION

There are many crowdsourcing ideas. Have students search for Zooniverse (https://www.zooniverse.org) for crowdsourcing projects, or for Tribewanted to view their recent projects. Have them choose one project that they would like to join and research it. Have them create a chart that shows the pros and cons of the project. Then have them work in groups of three or four to explain the project they selected and try to convince the other members of their group to join them. Have the group vote on the project they most want to join.

Writing

OVERVIEW

In this section, students prepare to write a paragraph about crowdsourcing. The lesson starts by teaching students how to use the present perfect tense. Students then learn how to write a concluding sentence. In the *Writing Task*, students apply these lessons by brainstorming, planning, and writing about the project. As added support, they will encounter two drafts of sample paragraphs and revising strategies that the author used. Students will use a checklist to revise their own paragraphs. Editing practice helps students correct common mistakes with the present perfect tense. After this, students write the final drafts of their paragraphs.

EXPLORING WRITTEN ENGLISH (pages 55–57)

A Noticing

This exercise is to be done before going over the information in the *Language for Writing* box. If students feel this exercise is confusing, reassure them that they will learn more about it later.
- Have students complete the task individually.
- Have students check their answers in pairs.
- Check answers as a class.

Language for Writing: Using the Present Perfect Tense

The *Language for Writing* box describes how to form the present perfect tense. To begin, give some contrasting examples of sentences using the present perfect tense and the simple past tense. For example: *I have written many e-mails in my life. I have written three e-mails since lunchtime. I wrote three e-mails yesterday.* Have students read the text in the *Language for Writing* box aloud. Elicit reasons for using the present perfect tense (the action began in the past and continues in the present) and signal words, such as *since* and *recently*, which can help students recognize and use the present perfect tense.

B Language for Writing

Students practice forming the present perfect tense by completing the sentences.
- Allow students time to complete the activity individually.
- Have them check answers in pairs.
- Check answers as a class. Ask which verbs are irregular.

C Language for Writing

Students create their own sentences using the present perfect tense to discuss how they use the Internet and how it has affected their lives. Before beginning the exercise, remind students that they should look up past participles to make sure they have the correct form of the verb.
- Allow students time to complete the task individually.
- Read sentences in groups of three or four. Have the group check the grammar and then choose the three sentences to write on the board.
- Compare and correct the sentences on the board as a class.

> **Ideas for… EXPANSION**
>
> Have each student write four sentences, three true and one false, about themselves. Each sentence should demonstrate the present perfect tense. Encourage each student to use information that others might not know. Have students work in groups of three or four and read their sentences aloud. The other members of the group should try to guess which sentence is false.

See Grammar Summary on page 221 of the Student Book for additional practice with using the present perfect tense.

Writing Skill: Writing a Concluding Sentence

The *Writing Skill box* describes the importance of writing a good concluding sentence. It discusses the three common types of conclusions: to make a prediction, give an opinion, or restate the main idea. Elicit that a concluding sentence should be interesting, but it should not include any new or surprising information. Have students read the *Writing Skill box* aloud. Ask students which of these types of concluding sentences they usually use.

D Writing Skill

Students find the concluding statements in the reading passages and identify the types of concluding statements.

- Allow students time to complete the task individually.
- Have students check answers in pairs
- Check answers as a class. Ask students to note where these are in the passages.

E Writing Skill

Students write a concluding sentence for each paragraph.

- Have students complete the task individually.
- Have students form pairs and compare their answers.
- Discuss answers as a class. Write examples on the board and compare them.

ANSWER KEY

WRITING SKILL

D **1.** R (See page 49.)

    2. P (See page 53, Paragraph A.)

    3. O (See page 53, Paragraph B.)

E Answers will vary. Possible answers:

    1. More face-to-face contact with your loved ones will make you feel happier.

    2. In summary, reading the news online has many advantages over getting the news from other sources.

WRITING TASK *(page 58)*

40 MINS

A Taking Notes

Remind students that brainstorming is an important step for gathering ideas before writing. Read the text in the *Goal* box aloud so students will be familiar with the writing task before brainstorming.

- Allow time for students to look online and take notes individually. Provide assistance as needed.

- Have students share their ideas in pairs and offer feedback to each other.

B Planning

Students follow steps 1 to 3 to complete their outlines. Have a student read the steps aloud. Remind students that complete sentences are not necessary for the purpose, how it works, and what it has accomplished. It is more important to focus on organizing their information.

- Allow time for students to complete their outlines individually. Provide assistance as needed.

C First Draft

Have students write first drafts of their paragraphs based on their outlines.

- Allow time for students to complete the task individually. Provide assistance as needed. Refrain from error correction at this point.

ANSWER KEY

WRITING TASK

A Answers will vary. Possible answers: Tribewanted: founders = Ben Keene and Mark James; 2006—project started; learned about a project to help develop an island in Fiji; environmentally friendly volunteers; very successful

B Answers will vary. Possible answers:

Topic Sentence: Members of Tribewanted.com have collaborated to create virtual and real-life communities all over the world.

Purpose: to get members to meet and work together to help a community in need

How it works: People sign up online; members go to the island and work with the local people.

What it has accomplished so far: planted crops; set up environmentally friendly power sources on the island; expanded to other locations

Concluding Sentence: The website has successfully brought together people from very different cultures to form a real-world tribe.

REVISING PRACTICE *(page 59)*

The *Revising Practice* box contains an exercise that demonstrates several ways students can improve their first drafts.

- Allow time for students to analyze the two drafts and complete the exercise.
- Check answers as a class. Ask students to identify each change and explain how it makes the revised draft stronger.

D Revised Draft

Students should apply the revision techniques used in the *Revising Practice box* to their own drafts, where applicable.

- Explain to students that they will be using the questions as a guide for checking and improving their drafts.
- As a class, go over the questions carefully to make sure students understand them.
- Allow students time to revise their paragraphs.

EDITING PRACTICE *(page 60)*

The *Editing Practice* box trains students to spot and correct common errors related to the present perfect tense. As a class, go over the information in the box carefully.

- Allow students time to complete the exercise individually.
- Check answers in pairs.
- Check answers as a class by asking students to read their corrected sentences aloud and explain the errors.

Ideas for… EXPANSION

Editing codes are helpful devices to use when commenting on students' work. Using these codes helps students correct their own work. Make a list of the codes you use on the board. Write sentences with one error each, and elicit the error. (Examples: She have three sisters [SV]. *or* The techer is funny [SP].) Have students copy the codes in their notebooks. They can refer to them when you return their work to them. Some example codes: SP (spelling), T (tense), WW (wrong word), ^ (missing word), WF (word form), SV (subject-verb agreement), WO (word order)

E Final Draft

Have students apply the skills taught in *Editing Practice* to their own revised drafts and check for any other errors.

- Allow time for students to work individually on editing their drafts.
- Walk around and monitor students as they work. Provide assistance as needed.
- Collect their work once they have completed it.
- For the next class, show anonymous examples of good paragraphs and common errors.

UNIT REVIEW

Students can work in groups on this recap of the unit. For question **1**, encourage students to use the target words when appropriate. For questions **2** and **3**, encourage them to check the relevant pages of the unit for answers.

- Allow students time to answer the three questions in groups.
- As a class, have students share their answers to question **1**. Have them vote on the project they would most like to join.

SAVING OUR SEAS

ACADEMIC TRACK
Environmental Science

ACADEMIC SKILLS
READING	Interpreting visual information
WRITING	Explaining a chart or graph
GRAMMAR	Describing charts and graphs
CRITICAL THINKING	Evaluating an argument

UNIT OVERVIEW

The theme of this unit is ocean conservation. The unit discusses the changes in fishing that have had consequences for many different fish populations in oceans and seas and the impact this has had on the environment. It provides a closer look at bluefin tuna and explains how we can help to minimize the impact of human activity.

- **READING 1:** This reading passage discusses overfishing in the world's seas and oceans and its impact on the oceans.

- **VIDEO:** A Japanese scientist, Shukei Masuma, is breeding bluefin tuna in captivity in an effort to save the species.

- **READING 2:** A chef and conservationist, Barton Seaver, discusses how fishing for top predators affects the food chain, which can lead to consequences for all of us.

Students draw on what they've read and watched to write a paragraph describing a graph or chart. The unit prepares them by introducing vocabulary to talk about ocean conservation, reviewing language to talk about charts and graphs, and offering tips for evaluating sources of information. Lastly, students practice brainstorming and using an outline to prepare drafts—skills that they will use in every unit's *Writing Task*.

⏱ 5 MINS THINK AND DISCUSS *(page 61)*

The questions help prepare students for the subject matter covered in the unit—ocean conservation.

- Have students study the picture, title, and caption.
- Discuss the photo as a class. Ask students: Have you ever been diving? Would you like to go? Why or why not?
- Discuss the two questions as a class. For question **2**, make a list on the board of the seafood that students like to eat.

THINK AND DISCUSS

Answers will vary. Possible answers:

1. The Atlantic Ocean is close to my home. I see it every day, because my house is on the coast.

2. I don't eat seafood. There isn't a good reason why I don't eat it. I just don't like the taste!

⏱ 15 MINS EXPLORE THE THEME *(pages 62–63)*

The opening spread features a map that shows the impact that human activities have on oceans around the world. It also has descriptions of four of the world's seas and the problems that they face.

- Before students answer the questions, ask them to look at the pictures and guess what problems will be mentioned.
- Allow time for students to study the spread and answer the questions individually.
- Have students check answers in pairs.
- Discuss answers as a class. For question **1**, ask students whether the levels of impact in the spread reflect their own experiences. For question **2**, ask volunteers to summarize the information about the four places mentioned. Can they think of other problems with pollution?
- Elicit example sentences from students for each of the ~~blue~~ *yellow* words.

EXPLORE THE THEME

A 1. The map shows the impact that humans have had on the world's oceans. The colors indicate the level of impact of human activity (ranging from very high to very low).

 2. Answers will vary. Possible answers: Fish are disappearing; there are "dead zones" without enough oxygen; water becomes more acidic. Other problems include rising water temperatures and overfishing.

B commercial

 survive

 species (Note: The word *species* is used for both the singular and plural forms. There can be one species or three species.)

Reading 1

30 MINS **PREPARING TO READ** *(page 64)*

A Building Vocabulary

The seven words in the box are key vocabulary items that appear in the passage. Students should use contextual clues to deduce the meanings of the words and complete the definitions.

- Have students complete the exercise individually.
- Check answers as a class.
- Elicit sample sentences for each vocabulary item. Ask: Is there a diverse student population at this school? Would you like to reduce or double the amount of homework you have?

See Vocabulary Extension 4A on page 206 of the Student Book for additional practice with Word Forms: Changing Nouns into Adjectives.

B Using Vocabulary

Students should practice using the new vocabulary items while answering the three questions. Point out that this provides practice with vocabulary from *Explore the Theme* as well.

- Have students work in pairs to answer the questions.
- Check answers as a class. Elicit example answers from students. For question **1**, ask students how long they estimate humans and fish can go without air/water. For question **2**, ask which species they would most like to see in the wild. For question **3**, ask how much trash they estimate that their families create every week.

C Predicting

Students skim the reading passage to make their own guesses about this reading. Point out that skimming means allowing your eyes to move quickly over the words. One skimming strategy is to read the first sentence of each paragraph.

- Have students skim the material. Give a time limit of 1 to 2 minutes.
- Have them discuss their answers in pairs.
- Discuss the most probable answers as a class. Ask students whether they tried the strategy of reading the first sentences. Ask them to provide one word to describe the topic of this passage. Revisit this question after completing the reading.

ANSWER KEY

PREPARING TO READ

A **1.** reduce

2. restore

3. estimate (Note: This is the same word for the verb or the noun.)

4. diverse

5. stable

6. quantity

7. doubled

B   Answers will vary. Possible answers:

1. Fish need water, oxygen, the correct temperature, and food—either plants or other animals. Humans need water, oxygen, food, shelter, and sleep.

2. dolphins, seals, octopi, squid, mussels, whales

3. by recycling, taking public transportation, using renewable energy, and not littering

C   1, 3, 6

 1.07 Have students read the passage individually, or play the audio and have students read along.

OVERVIEW OF THE READING

The reading passage presents some of the causes and effects of overfishing in the world's oceans. It warns that many more fish could disappear and suggests some possible solutions to the problem.

Online search terms: Overfishing Science; Pristine Seas; Census of Marine Life

40 MINS **UNDERSTANDING THE READING** *(page 67)*

A Understanding Main Ideas

Students are asked to identify the main idea for each of the sections of the reading passage.

- Allow students time to complete the activity individually.
- Check answers as a class. Ask students how they arrived at their answers.

B Understanding a Process

Students test their understanding of the details in the passage by completing the diagram with the words from the box. Draw the diagram on the board, and elicit the first answer (dropped) as an example.

- Allow students time to complete the diagram individually.
- Have them check their answers in pairs.
- Discuss answers as a class. Complete the diagram on the board.

C Identifying Problems and Solutions

Students should reread the section *A Future for Fish*? in the reading passage and find the three solutions. Students do not need to write full sentences for each answer.

- Allow students time to complete the task individually.
- Have students compare their answers in pairs.
- Check answers as a class. Ask volunteers to give their solutions.

D Critical Thinking: Evaluating an Argument

The *Critical Thinking* box explains how to evaluate an argument by looking for facts and statistics that the author uses to support their argument. Students should read the reading passage again to note what statistics the author has used to make the argument against overfishing.

- Have students discuss their answers in pairs.
- Discuss answers as a class. Draw a T-chart on the board with statistics in the article and statistics that students think should be included. Fill in the chart based on students' ideas. Ask students whether what they have learned from this reading will affect their own eating habits. Why or why not?

Ideas for... EXPANSION

Have students choose an ocean species to research online. They should create a pamphlet with the following information:

What does the species look like?

Where does it live?

Who are its predators?

Who is its prey?

Is this species in danger? Why or why not?

UNDERSTANDING THE READING

A **Source of the Problem:** b (Explanation: Option a is false.)

Rise of the Little Fish: b (Explanation: Option a is false.)

A Future for Fish?: a (Explanation: Option b is not mentioned.)

B **1.** dropped

2. too few

3. increased

4. Too many

C Answers will vary. Possible answers:

1. Commercial fishing companies shouldn't catch so many large fish.

2. Develop fish farming (aquaculture).

3. Don't eat overfished species; eat farmed fish instead.

D **1.** In 2010, the Census of Marine Life estimated that 90% of the big ocean fish populations are gone. Small fish (e.g., sardines and anchovies) have more than doubled in number. If we continue to overfish the oceans, scientists predict that most of the fish that we catch now will disappear by 2050.

2. Answers will vary. Possible answers:
I think this argument would be more convincing if the writer provided more statistics—e.g., the amount of fish currently produced through aquaculture, the amount of fish caught per week through commercial fishing, the population of bluefin tuna today.

DEVELOPING READING SKILLS *(page 68)*

Reading Skill: Interpreting Visual Information

The *Reading Skill* box explains that authors use visual materials to help the reader see a lot of information quickly. Ask students whether they usually look at graphs and diagrams while reading an article. Why or why not? Explain that graphs and diagrams can help students evaluate an argument by providing more statistics to support an idea. Ask students to look at the graph. What does the x-axis show? What does the y-axis show? Explain that this information is important to notice when they are reading a graph.

A Interpreting Graphs

Students should look at the graph to answer the questions. Elicit the answer for the first question (What does the graph show? What do the colors represent?), and ask students where they found this answer.

- Allow time for students to complete the task individually.
- Have students check answers in pairs.
- Discuss answers as a class. Ask volunteers to explain how they arrived at their answers. Ask students what other information they noticed in the graph. Ask whether anything surprised them.

B Interpreting Maps

Students should look back at the *Explore and Discuss* world map on pages 62 and 63 to answer these questions.

- Have students complete the task in pairs.
- Discuss answers as a class. Ask students for possible reasons *why* these places are the most and least affected by human activity.

ANSWER KEY

DEVELOPING READING SKILLS

A 1. The graph shows the historical annual catch of Pacific bluefin tuna by country from 1952 to 2012. The colors represent countries that catch the fish.

2. Japan and the United States

3. approximately 15,000 metric tons

4. lowest—1990; highest—1956

B 1. The North Sea and the East China Sea

2. Antarctica and the North Pole / the North and South Poles

Video

40 MINS VIEWING: SAVING BLUEFIN TUNA *(pages 69–70)*

Overview of the Video

This video is about a Japanese scientist who is trying to breed bluefin tuna in captivity. It is quite difficult to create conditions in which this type of fish can breed, but he has been successful. After the fish are hatched, he returns them to the ocean. He hopes this will help to prevent the bluefin tuna from becoming extinct.

Online search terms: bluefin tuna; Shukei Masuma; sustainable sushi;

BEFORE VIEWING

A Learning About the Topic

The paragraph prepares students for the video by giving them background information about three species of bluefin tuna.

- Have students complete the task individually.
- Discuss answers as a class. Elicit example answers. Ask students whether they have ever eaten bluefin tuna. Are they surprised to learn that the fish is in danger? Why or why not?

B Vocabulary in Context

This exercise introduces students to some of the key words used in the video.

- Have students complete the task individually.
- Check answers as a class. Ask students how they think these words might be used in the video.

ANSWER KEY

BEFORE VIEWING

A 1. They are big and can swim very fast.

2. People like to eat bluefin tuna as sushi or sashimi.

3. Answers will vary. Possible answers: breed more bluefin tuna on fish farms; put a quota on the number of bluefin tuna caught in the sea; stop eating bluefin tuna.

B 1. hatchling (Note: The verb *hatch* describes the process of emerging from an egg. Baby birds and turtles are also called hatchlings.)

2. captivity

3. breed

WHILE VIEWING

Ⓐ ▶ Understanding the Main Idea

Have students read the items silently before you play the video.

- Have them complete the task while the video is playing.
- Check the answer as a class. Discuss why the other statements are incorrect.

Ⓑ ▶ Understanding Details

Have students read the paragraph and circle the words that they recall from the first viewing before playing the video a second time.

- Have students complete the task while the video is playing.
- Check answers as a class. Ask a volunteer to read the paragraph aloud.

AFTER VIEWING

Ⓐ Interpreting Graphs

Students are asked to reflect on the information in the video and study the graph. Direct students to the Reading Skill on page 68 for help with interpreting visual information.

- Have students discuss the questions in pairs.
- Check answers as a class. Ask when the Pacific bluefin tuna population was at its peak. Ask students why the Pacific bluefin tuna population might have dropped in number before the Atlantic. Then ask volunteers to share what else they notice about the graph.

Ideas for… EXPANSION

As a class, make a list of endangered species on the board. Then ask students which species they would choose to breed in captivity. Have students form pairs and explain that they should:

1. Choose an animal they are both interested in protecting. Have them write some brief reasons why they want to protect this animal.

2. Brainstorm what they know about this animal and create a word web on paper. What will they need for their project?

3. Create a visual representation of their breeding project. What would they need to create this environment for the animals? Students will need to decide how much land is required, and draw a building plan showing the layout of the enclosures, pools, and other structures.

4. If computers are available, have students search online to find out more about the endangered species they have chosen and whether breeding programs already exist. Ask students to make improvements to their plans if appropriate. Encourage students to bookmark any charts or graphs they find online, because they may want to use these for this unit's writing task.

5. Have students share their plans with the class. Ask students to compare the breeding projects. Which ones seem most realistic? What do the projects have in common? If possible, post the plans around the class and allow time for students to read their classmates' work.

Reading 2

PREPARING TO READ *(page 71)*

A Building Vocabulary

In this exercise, students complete sentences that follow the same topic as the reading passage. Explain that the sentences in the box define the blue words. Remind students to use the correct forms of the words.

- Allow time for students to complete the exercise individually.
- Have students check their answers in pairs.
- Check answers as a class. Elicit example sentences for each vocabulary item. Ask students to name one individual they can always rely on. Also ask: Are population numbers declining where you live? Why or why not? What is something that you will definitely do after class today?

See Vocabulary Extension 4B on page 206 of the Student Book for additional practice with Word Partners: verb + on.

B Using Vocabulary

Students should use the new vocabulary items while discussing the three questions.

- Have students work in pairs to answer the questions.
- Discuss answers as a class. Elicit example answers from students.

C Brainstorming

This exercise gets students thinking about what they can do to keep oceans healthy. Ideas should be brief. Draw a word web on the board with the words "healthy oceans" and a sample answer (raise awareness).

- Allow time for students write their answers individually.
- Have students compare their ideas in pairs.
- Ask for volunteers to share their answers, and write the words and phrases on a word web on the board.

ANSWER KEY

PREPARING TO READ

A 1. individuals (Note: Using the word *individuals* as a plural noun means that there are many individuals who are recognized as different people, not as one large group.)

2. declining; definitely

3. essential (Note: If something *dies out*, it means that the species has become extinct.)

4. informed

5. severe

6. impact

7. rely on

B Answers will vary. Possible answers:

1. clean air; protected areas for wildlife; balanced ecosystems

2. I read articles, listen to lectures, and watch nature shows.

3. rising sea levels; unstable weather patterns

C Answers will vary. Possible answers:

raise awareness about overfishing; donate to charities that protect the oceans; help clean up beaches; make informed choices about seafood; eat farmed fish

---

 1.08 Have students read the passage individually, or play the audio and have students read along.

OVERVIEW OF THE READING

The reading passage is an interview with a chef and conservationist, Barton Seaver. His recommendations include making better food choices when we eat, eating farm-raised fish, eating fish that are low on the food chain, and thinking more about our relationship with our environment.

Online search terms: Barton Seaver Projects; Barton Seaver TED Talk; Seafood decision guide; National Geographic Overfishing

UNDERSTANDING THE READING *(page 74)*

A Understanding the Main Idea

Students choose the sentence that best summarizes Seaver's message.

- Have students complete the task individually.
- Check answers as a class.

B Identifying Opinions

Students are asked to decide whether Seaver would agree with these statements. Explain that some of the topics are not discussed in the interview. Students should circle NG (not given) for these statements.

- Allow time for students to complete the task individually.
- Check answers as a class. Ask students where they found the answers in the reading.

C Interpreting Visual Information

Have students read the passage and look at the illustration to find the answers to the questions. Remind students to read the introductory paragraph and the explanations of the different levels of ocean species. Ask students which species they already know. Which ones are new to them?

- Allow time for students to complete the rest of the task individually.
- Check answers as a class.

D Critical Thinking: Synthesizing

Have students look again on pages 72 and 73 for the information in the illustrations.

- Allow students time to answer the questions individually.
- Have students share their answers with a partner.
- Discuss as a class. Make a T-chart with OK and AVOID on the board. Elicit example answers, and write these in the T-chart.

Ideas for… EXPANSION

Have students make a list of seafood that they usually eat. (Remind them that this was one of the questions at the beginning of the unit.) If computers are available, have students go online to http://ocean.nationalgeographic.com/take-action/seafood-decision-guide/. Have them click on different fish and find out whether they are sustainable. If these are not good fish choices, what alternatives could students choose? Have students form pairs and make a list of three to five sustainable fish that they would like to eat. If students do not eat fish, have them choose three to five fish that they would recommend serving at a restaurant.

E Critical Thinking: Reflecting

Have students reflect on what they have learned in this unit and connect this with their own eating habits.

- Have students share their ideas with a partner Ask whether they agree or disagree with each other.
- Discuss as a class. Elicit example answers.

ANSWER KEY

UNDERSTANDING THE READING

A c (Explanation: Seaver says that people can continue to eat seafood, so option a is wrong. Although he says that the ocean provides an important part of our diet, this is not his main message, so option b is not the correct answer. Seaver wants people to think about their seafood choices, so the correct answer is option c.)

B 1. Y (Paragraph B)
 2. N (Paragraph B)
 3. NG
 4. Y (Paragraph C)
 5. NG
 6. N (Paragraph D)
 7. Y (Paragraph E)

C 1. Answers will vary. Possible answers: Atlantic bluefin tuna; orange roughy; Atlantic salmon
 2. carnivores
 3. an animal that eats plants
 4. anchovies
 5. Answers will vary. Possible answers: Alaska pollock; Atlantic herring
 6. because they make their own food and produce all the oxygen in the ocean (Note: The answer to this question is not in the illustration. It's in Paragraph F.)

D Answers will vary. Possible answers:

Fish that are OK to eat: Alaska pollock; Atlantic herring; Japanese flying squid; American lobster; anchovies

Fish we should avoid: Atlantic bluefin tuna; orange roughy; Atlantic salmon

E Answers will vary. Possible answers:

This unit has definitely made me think about my eating choices. I'll try to eat more farmed fish from now on to protect the ocean's ecosystem.

Writing

OVERVIEW

In this section, students prepare to write a paragraph describing a chart or graph. The lesson starts by teaching students language that can be used to describe charts and graphs. Students then learn how to explain a chart or graph, starting with the main idea or purpose. In the *Writing Task*, students apply these lessons by brainstorming, planning, and writing about a graph. As added support, they will encounter two drafts of sample paragraphs and revising strategies that the author used. Students will use a checklist to revise their own paragraphs. Editing practice helps students correct common mistakes with prepositions, verbs used to describe trends, and the past tense. After this, students write the final drafts of their paragraphs.

 EXPLORING WRITTEN ENGLISH
(pages 75–77)

A Noticing

Students are expected to notice the language to describe upward and downward trends. Explain that a trend is a change or development toward something new or different. This exercise is to be done before going over the information in the *Language for Writing* box. Do the first sentence as an example with the class. Elicit that this must be DT (downward trend) because the amount "has fallen."

- Allow time for students to complete the task individually.
- Check answers as a class. Ask students how they arrived at their answers. Explain that the *Language for Writing* box will provide more details about these trends.

Language for Writing: Describing Charts and Graphs

The *Language for Writing* box reviews words that are used to describe charts and graphs, including phrases to introduce a description and common verbs and prepositions that are used to talk about changes and developments. Have students circle the verbs in exercise **A** that show whether the trend has been upward, downward, or stable. Have them underline the phrases that introduce the sentence and draw a square around each preposition.

B Language for Writing

Students practice using the information in the box by completing the sentences about the graph.
- Allow students time to complete the activity individually.
- Have them check answers in pairs.
- Check answers as a class.

C Language for Writing

Students write sentences about the graph on page 70. Refer students to the *Language for Writing* box for help writing these sentences.
- Allow students time to complete the task individually.
- Have students compare their answers in pairs.
- Check answers as a class. Elicit example sentences from students, and write them on the board.

ANSWER KEY

EXPLORING WRITTEN ENGLISH

A 1. DT
2. UT
3. NC
4. UT
5. DT

LANGUAGE FOR WRITING

B 1. increased
2. doubled
3. remained stable

C Answers will vary. Possible answers:
1. In the early 1960s, the Pacific bluefin population peaked at approximately 140,000 metric tons.
2. Between 1961 and 1974, the Pacific bluefin tuna population decreased dramatically.
3. As the graph shows, the Pacific bluefin population rose to almost 50,000 metric tons by 1992.

Writing Skill: Explaining a Chart or Graph

The *Writing Skill* box explains that descriptions of charts or graphs begin by explaining the main idea or purpose and then providing facts (specific information) to support this main idea. Have a student read each of the main idea examples in the box followed by the supporting detail. Ask students to note which is more specific— the main idea or the supporting detail.

D Writing Skill

Students look at the graph and then decide whether the statements correctly reflect the information. Remind students to pay attention to the x- and y-axes and the key.

- Allow students time to complete the task individually.
- Have students check their answers in pairs.

E Writing Skill

Students read the sentences for exercise **D** again and correct the incorrect statements, using the information in the graph.

- Allow students time to complete the task individually.
- Check answers as a class.

F Writing Skill

Students should refer to the information in the *Writing Skill* box to write a paragraph about the graph. Remind students to pay attention to transition words to help them organize the sentences into a paragraph.

- Allow time for students to complete the task individually. Walk around, and provide assistance as needed.
- Check answers as a class. Ask volunteers to read their versions of the paragraph aloud. Have students explain how they arrived at their answers.

ANSWER KEY

WRITING SKILL

D   1, 2, 5

E 3. In 2005, total bluefin production was almost <u>90,000</u> metric tons; by 2009, that number had fallen to about 60,000.

  4. According to the graph, total production of bluefin tuna <u>decreased</u> steadily between 2005 and 2009.

F   The graph shows global production for each species of bluefin tuna in metric tons per year. According to the graph, total production of bluefin tuna decreased steadily between 2005 and 2009. In 2005, total bluefin production was almost 90,000 metric tons; by 2009, that number had fallen to about 60,000. As for production level by species, both Atlantic and Pacific bluefin tuna showed some variation between 2005 and 2009. However, production of Southern bluefin tuna remained more or less stable.

WRITING TASK *(page 78)*

A Planning

Remind students that planning is an *essential* step for gathering ideas before writing. Read the *Goal* box aloud so students will be familiar with the writing task before planning. If possible, have students bring in graphs from outside sources, such as magazines, newspapers, or the Internet, that they would like to use. Emphasize that the graphs do not have to be about ocean conservation. They can be about any topic that has changed over time. Students can also use one of the graphs in this book. Remind students that complete sentences are not necessary. It is more important to focus on organizing the information.

- Allow time for students to complete their outlines individually. Provide assistance as needed.

B First Draft

Have students write first drafts of their paragraphs based on their outlines. Make sure that students have a copy of the chart or graph available while they work on this.

- Allow time for students to complete the task individually. Provide assistance as needed. Refrain from error correction at this point.

ANSWER KEY

WRITING TASK

A   Answers will vary. Possible answers:

  Main idea: Housing prices have increased in every neighborhood in the city.

  Detail: Housing prices in Jamaica Plain and the North End doubled between 2010 and 2014.

  Most recent piece of data: Housing prices in Roxbury increased by 60% in the 7-year period.

REVISING PRACTICE *(page 79)*

The *Revising Practice* box contains an exercise that demonstrates several ways students can improve their first drafts.

- Allow time for students to analyze the two drafts and complete the exercise.
- Check answers as a class. Ask students to identify each change and explain how it makes the revised draft stronger.

C Revised Draft

Students should apply the revision techniques used in the *Revising Practice* box to their own drafts, where applicable.

- Explain to students that they will be using the questions as a guide for checking and improving their drafts.
- As a class, go over the questions carefully to make sure students understand them.
- Allow students time to revise their paragraphs.

EDITING PRACTICE *(page 80)*

The *Editing Practice* box trains students to spot and correct common errors related to describing a chart or graph. As a class, go over the information in the box carefully to make sure students understand what to look out for.

- Allow students time to complete the exercise individually.
- Check answers as a class by asking students to read their corrected sentences aloud and explain the errors.

ANSWER KEY

REVISING PRACTICE

d, c, a, b

EDITING PRACTICE

1. As we can see from the <u>graph, global</u> aquaculture production of Atlantic salmon was stable between 1950 and 1980.
2. Production of Atlantic salmon doubled <u>between</u> 1990 and 1995.
3. Between 1991 and 1992, production of Atlantic salmon <u>declined</u> slightly.
4. Between 1999 and 2001, production of Atlantic salmon <u>grew</u> by about 200,000 metric tons.
5. Production of Atlantic salmon decreased slightly <u>in</u> 2009.

D Final Draft

Have students apply the skills taught in *Editing Practice* to their own revised drafts and check for any other errors.

- Allow time for students to work individually on editing their drafts.
- Walk around, and monitor students as they work. Provide assistance as needed.
- Collect their work once they have completed it.
- For the next class, show anonymous examples of good paragraphs and common errors.

 UNIT REVIEW

Students can work in groups on this recap of the unit. For question **1**, encourage students to use the target words when appropriate. For questions **2** and **3**, encourage them to check the relevant pages of the unit for answers.

- Allow students time to answer the two questions in groups. For question **1**, ask groups to decide which factors they think are most effective for restoring the ocean's biodiversity.
- Ask each group to present its answer for question **1**. Have students vote for what they believe is the most important factor.

ACADEMIC TRACK
Psychology/Biology

ACADEMIC SKILLS

READING	Identifying cause and effect
WRITING	Using an outline
GRAMMAR	Using *by* + gerund
CRITICAL THINKING	Applying a method

UNIT OVERVIEW

The theme of this unit is memory—its importance in ancient times and now, the loci method, the USA memory championships, tips and techniques for memorization, and the connection between memory and sleep.

- **READING 1:** The reading provides a look at the history of the loci method and the importance placed on memory in ancient times. It also discusses the reasons why memory is less valued today.

- **VIDEO:** An explanation of how a USA memory champion uses the loci method to quickly remember the order of a deck of cards.

- **READING 2:** The reading discusses the connection between memory and sleep. During deep sleep, brain waves help transform short-term memories to long-term memories. The reading also gives tips on improving memory.

Students draw on what they've read and watched to write a discussion paragraph about how to improve memory. The unit prepares them by introducing vocabulary to talk about memory, teaching how to use *by* + gerund, and offering tips for how to use an outline. The unit also explains how to identify cause and effect. Lastly, it introduces students to brainstorming and again using an outline to prepare drafts—skills that students will use in every unit's *Writing Task*.

THINK AND DISCUSS *(page 81)*

The questions help prepare students for the subject matter covered in the unit—memory and how it relates to learning. The scene depicts an artist, Stephen Wiltshire, drawing the New York City skyline from memory.

- Have students study the picture, title, and captions.
- Discuss the photo as a class. What do students think the photo and the unit are about? Provide your own overview.
- Discuss the two questions as a class. Ask students to reflect on their own lives. Do they have good memories? Who do they know with a good memory? What can these people remember?

ANSWER KEY

THINK AND DISCUSS

Answers will vary. Possible answers:

1. My earliest memory is my mother picking me up from my crib when I was about 3 years old.

2. I think some people have better memories because they focus more on what they are doing. But some people are better at remembering pictures, while others are better at remembering facts.

EXPLORE THE THEME *(pages 82–83)*

Students test their own memories and then analyze a graph depicting how memory changes with age.

- Allow students time to study the spread and answer question **1** individually. Time the class together.
- Have students discuss question **2** in pairs.
- Discuss answers as a class.
- Have students answer the question in part **B** in pairs. Remind students to use the vocabulary for describing graphs that they learned in unit 4.
- Have students complete part **C** individually. Remind students to use the correct forms of the words.
- Elicit example sentences from students for each of the blue words.

ANSWER KEY

EXPLORE THE THEME

A   Answers will vary.

B   Answers will vary. Possible answers: According to the graph, memory declines with age. Verbal recall actually increases slightly from the age of 16 to 32, but then declines steadily after that. Visual recall drops approximately 30 percent from the age of 48 to 80.

C   technique; gradually; complex

Reading 1

30 MINS PREPARING TO READ *(page 84)*

A Building Vocabulary

Students find the seven blue words in the passage and use contextual clues to guess the meanings of the words. Remind students to look for the parts of speech to help them better understand the new words.

- Allow time for students to complete the exercise individually.
- Check answers as a class. What clues from the reading passage did students find helpful?
- Elicit example sentences for each vocabulary item. Ask: What is an achievement that you are proud of? Can you visualize your bedroom when you close your eyes?

See Vocabulary Extension 5A on page 207 of the Student Book for additional practice with Word Forms: Changing Nouns and Adjectives into Verbs.

B Using Vocabulary

Students should practice using the new vocabulary items while answering the two questions.

- Have students discuss their answers in pairs.
- Compare answers as a class. Elicit example answers from students. For question **1**, ask students what they can remember about their partner's place. For question **2**, ask students why these external conditions make it difficult. What would an *internal* condition be?

C Classifying

Students complete the chart with their ideas. Each idea should be brief. Elicit examples before students begin.

- Have students work individually to complete the exercise.
- Have them compare answers in groups of three or four. Encourage students to explain *why* they chose their answers.
- Draw the T-chart on the board, and elicit answers from different groups in the class.

D Predicting

Students scan the passage to make their own guesses about this reading. Elicit strategies for scanning a reading passage. Students should let their eyes move quickly down the page, without worrying about unknown words. They can read the first paragraph, then scan the rest of the passage for similar words. Point out that answers will vary.

- Have students scan the reading for repeated words. Stress that students should not try to read the entire passage. Give students 1 minute for this activity, and time them, if possible.

- Have them discuss their answers in pairs.
- As a class, have volunteers share the words that they found. Then have students share their predictions. Revisit this question after the reading.

ANSWER KEY

PREPARING TO READ

A **1.** familiar; **2.** text; **3.** internal; **4.** external; **5.** visualize; **6.** memorize; **7.** achievement

B Answers will vary. Possible answers:

1. My kitchen is a place that is very familiar to me. It's a big room with a large wooden table and a green and white floor.

2. I find it difficult to study when people are talking on the phone or watching TV. I also find it difficult to study if the room is messy. I need a clean space to study well.

C Answers will vary. Possible answers:

Things I make lists for: food shopping; household chores; homework assignment due dates

Things I try to memorize: irregular verbs; history dates; passwords; locker combinations

D Answers will vary. Possible answers: technique, loci, visualize, remember

---

 1.09 Have students read the passage individually, or play the audio and have students read along.

OVERVIEW OF THE READING

The reading passage describes how attitudes toward memory have changed over the centuries; it also explains a special technique for memorization called the loci method.

Online search terms: Memory Palace; Joshua Foer TED Talk; Simonides

40 MINS UNDERSTANDING THE READING *(page 87)*

A Understanding the Main Idea

Students are asked to identify the main idea of the reading passage.

- Have students complete the activity individually.
- Check the answer as a class. Ask students how they arrived at the answer.

B Understanding Details

Students test their understanding of the details in the passage. Explain that a *task* is a small job or chore. If you *value* something, it means it is important to you.

- Allow students time to complete the questions individually.
- Have them check their answers in pairs.
- Check answers as a class. Ask students if anything surprised them about the information in this reading.

C Classifying

Students think about the techniques and decide whether these are internal or external. Ask students if they think that classifying items is a type of memory technique. Elicit the reasons why this can be helpful. Students may need the first item done as an example.

- Have students complete the task individually.
- Check answers as a class, and draw a T-chart on the board with the answers. Ask students to add additional internal and external memory devices to the list.

D Critical Thinking: Applying a Method

The *Critical Thinking* box explains that applying a new strategy to your own life can help you remember and understand it better. Have a student read the text in the *Critical Thinking* box aloud. Then have students try to use the loci method. Assure students that this is a difficult concept, and encourage them to reread paragraphs **B** and **C** on page 85.

- Have students discuss their answers in pairs.
- Discuss answers as a class. Elicit example answers. Ask students if they think they will use the loci method in the future. Why or why not?

E Critical Thinking: Reflecting

Have students think about the author's quote and reflect on their own experience. Encourage students to summarize the quote in their own words and answer the questions. Remind them to justify their opinions.

- Have students answer the questions individually
- Have students discuss their answers in pairs.
- Discuss answers as a class. Ask students whether they agree with their classmates. Why or why not? Ask students if they would be willing to give up the external memory devices in exercise C to improve their own memories.

ANSWER KEY

UNDERSTANDING THE READING

A   b (Explanation: The passage discusses memorization techniques from the past until now.)

B 1. Answers will vary. Possible answers: The loci method is a way to remember things by visualizing them in different areas of a place that you know well. (See paragraphs B and C.)

   2. He was able to memorize religious texts, poems, speeches, etc., and could take them everywhere he went, in his mind. (See paragraph D.)

   3. because most people didn't have books or pens to write notes with, so they had to remember things to preserve their society's cultural heritage (See paragraph E.)

   4. memorizing religious texts or myths and folktales (See paragraph F.)

C   **1.** I; **2.** E; **3.** E; **4.** I; **5.** E

D   Answers will vary. Possible answers:

   1. I'd separate the words by topic and visualize them around my kitchen. Words about memory could be in my refrigerator. Words about oceans could be near my stove because I cook fish!

   2. I'd picture my bedroom and create different areas for one name and one date. For example, 1066 is the date that William the Conqueror conquered England. I would visualize William by my desk, writing *1066*.

E   Answers will vary. Possible answers: Yes, I think we have lost an important skill. For example, we don't have to remember phone numbers now because we can store them in our phones. If we lose the phone, we may lose all the phone numbers, too.

DEVELOPING READING SKILLS *(page 88)*

Reading Skill: Identifying Cause and Effect

The *Reading Skill* box describes how to identify causes and effects. It explains the importance of identifying this information in order to understand a reading, and points out words that often signal this relationship. Have a student read the text in the box aloud. Write the two example sentences on the board, and circle the cause. Then underline the effect, and point out that either the cause or the effect clause can begin a sentence. Draw arrows from the cause to the effect to show the progression from one to the other. Have students rewrite the sentences with the clauses reversed. Remind them to change the signal words as well.

A Identifying Cause and Effect

Each of the memorization techniques contains a cause and an effect. Students should circle the causes and underline the effects. Remind students that the cause can come before or after the effect. Note that the initial *m* in the word *mnemonic* is silent.

- Allow time for students to complete the task individually.
- Have students check answers in pairs.

- Discuss answers as a class. Brainstorm words with *ie* or *ei*, and write them on the board. (Examples: *believe, achieve, ceiling, deceive.* Exceptions to the rule: *seize, leisure.*) Ask students to identify the signal words used in the techniques.

B Identifying Cause and Effect

Students read the reading passage on pages 85–86 again and look for three causes and effects. Remind students to look for signal words.

- Allow students time to reread the passage and find their answers individually.
- Have them compare their answers in pairs.
- Discuss answers as a class. Have students read the causes and effects that they found aloud. Create a list of the signal words on the board.

ANSWER KEY

DEVELOPING READING SKILLS

A Five cause-effect relationships:

People often use mnemonics—like poems or pictures—because it's easier to remember rhymes or images than plain facts and lists.

… it may be hard to remember the colors of the rainbow in the order that they appear. Someone therefore made an acronym for this: ROY G BIV.

The name Roy G. Biv is meaningless, but it's short, so it's easier to remember than the list.

English spelling rules can also be difficult to learn, so some students use rhymes to help them remember the rules. By learning "*i* before *e* except after *c* (where you hear *ee*)," students of English can remember the spelling of words like *niece* and *receipt.*

B Answers will vary. Possible answers:

By using the loci method, he was able to "read" books stored in his memory palaces. (Paragraph D)

A person with a good memory was special because they could help preserve the society's cultural heritage. (Paragraph E)

We've invented devices so we don't have to store information in our brains. (Paragraph G)

Video

VIEWING: HOUSE OF CARDS
40 MINS
(pages 89–90)

Overview of the Video

The video shows how a memory champion memorizes the order of a deck of cards. He uses a memory palace and assigns each card a person, an action, and an object to help him with the process.

Online search terms: USA Memory Championship; World Memory Championships; memory sports

BEFORE VIEWING

A Learning about the Topic

The paragraph prepares students for the video by giving them background information about the USA Memory Championships.

- Have students complete the task individually.
- Discuss answers as a class. For question **1**, ask students how close their guesses were to the correct answer. For question **2**, elicit example answers from the class. Ask students if they think they would do well in this contest.

B Vocabulary in Context

This exercise introduces students to some of the key words used in the video. Remind students to try to infer the meaning from context. Point out that the part of speech for each of these words differs, so these clues can help to determine the meanings.

- Have students complete the task individually.
- Check answers as a class. Elicit example sentences for each word. Ask: Do you have a mental map of your school? What colors are associated with your country? Have you ever created a secret code with friends?

ANSWER KEY

BEFORE VIEWING

A 1. Answers will vary. Correct answer: 18.65 seconds

2. Answers will vary. Possible answer: They could connect the cards with objects around a living room and attach the same number and suit of each card to that object. For example, a mirror on the wall could have 8 hearts on the frame, and it would be the 8 of hearts.

B 1. mental map

2. associated

3. code

WHILE VIEWING

A ▶ Understanding Main Ideas

Have students read the items silently before you play the video. Have students match the statements to the steps.

- Have students complete the task while the video is playing.
- Have students compare answers in pairs.
- Check answers as a class.

B ▶ Understanding Details

Have students fill in any labels that they recall from the first viewing before playing the video a second time. Draw students' attention to the example to help them better understand the exercise.

- Have students complete the task while the video is playing.
- Have students compare answers in pairs.
- Check answers as a class. If possible, project the image onto the board, and fill in the labels. Ask students if they were surprised by Dellis's memory palace. Why or why not? Ask them to discuss the benefits and drawbacks of this method.

ANSWER KEY

WHILE VIEWING

A   Step 1: b; Step 2: a; Step 3: e

B 1. girlfriend's

   2. sword

   3. dancing

   4. boss

AFTER VIEWING

A Reacting to the Video

Students are asked to reflect on the information in the video.

- Have students discuss the question in pairs. Ask students: What kinds of images would you have in your own memory palace? Do you think your memory palace would look as strange or unusual?
- Allow time for the students to answer the question in pairs.
- As a class, ask for volunteers to share their answers.

B Critical Thinking: Applying a Method

Students draw on information from Reading 1 and the video to apply the techniques to their own lives. First, ask students whether they have difficulty remembering names. Why or why not?

- Allow students time to answer the questions in pairs.
- Discuss as a class. Elicit example answers, and write them on the board. Ask the class which of these methods they think would work the best.

Ideas for… EXPANSION

In groups of three or four, have students create lists of 20 famous people. These can be politicians, celebrities, authors, artists, etc. Have each group give its list to a different group. The group then takes the list and decides what strategies they will use to memorize it. Give the students 5 minutes to use their chosen method to memorize the list. Then collect the lists, and give everyone in the class 2 to 3 minutes to write down the people's names on the list in the correct order. Each student should work on this individually. Afterward, see who has remembered the most names on the list. Ask this student what strategy they used.

Ideas for… EXPANSION

In groups of three or four, have students use what they have learned about the loci method to create an advertisement (either on paper or in a short video) for a workshop for people who want to improve their memories. They should explain *why* this is important, describe the process itself, and provide a detailed example of a memory palace. Encourage students to make these advertisements persuasive for their audience. When they have completed the assignment, they should present their advertisements to the class.

ANSWER KEY

AFTER VIEWING

A   Answers will vary. Possible answer: Strange or unusual images are more memorable, so they are easier to recall. These images may seem strange to us, but they all have meaning for Dellis. These images are very personal to him based on his life experiences.

B   Answers will vary. Possible answer: I'd use a method of association. As I meet each person, I'd try to find an unusual feature—ears, forehead, eyebrows, eyes, nose, mouth, etc. Then I would form an association between this characteristic and the person's name.

Reading 2

PREPARING TO READ *(page 91)*

A Building Vocabulary

In this exercise, students read the definitions for eight words and then complete sentences that follow the same topic as the reading passage. Point out that students need to use the correct forms of the words.

- Have students complete the exercise individually.
- Check answers as a class. Elicit example sentences for each vocabulary item. Ask: What causes you stress? What happens when you need to transfer schools? Is there proof that aliens exist?"

See Vocabulary Extension 5B on page 207 of the Student Book for additional practice with Word Partners: Expressions with state.

B Using Vocabulary

Students should use the new vocabulary items while discussing the two questions.

- Have students work in pairs to answer the questions.
- Discuss answers as a class. Elicit example answers from students. Ask: What do you think is important for physical fitness? What route do you take to school each day?

C Predicting

Students predict the content of the reading passage by focusing on key words. Remind students that key words are words that are important, and are often repeated or follow a similar theme.

- Allow time for students to read the title and skim through the reading for the subheads. Students should write their answers individually.
- Have students work in pairs to compare their answers.
- Have students discuss their answers as a class. Discuss which words are repeated. Ask students to read the first paragraph and decide if this supports their ideas. Explain that they can check their prediction again after reading the entire passage.

🎧 **1.10** Have students read the passage individually, or play the audio and have students read along.

OVERVIEW OF THE READING

The reading passage explains how the brain transfers memories from the hippocampus to the neocortex while we sleep to create long-term memories. New research shows that brain waves occur during the deepest level of sleep, proving that sleep is important for learning and memory. There is also a section on other ways to improve memory, which mentions avoiding stress, playing games, and eating healthy food.

Online search terms: how sleep works; healthy sleep Harvard; be brain fit; the brain made simple

UNDERSTANDING THE READING *(page 94)*

A Understanding Main Ideas

Students check the sentences that are supported by the reading passage.

- Allow time for students to complete the task individually.
- Have students check answers in pairs.
- Check answers as a class. Ask students which statements they already knew and which ones are new. Ask whether they remember what the stages of sleep are called.

B Understanding a Process

Students complete the diagram with information from the reading passage. Point out that the arrows go clockwise. Elicit the meaning of *temporarily,* and explain that they will need to infer the information from what is written in the passage.

- Allow time for students to complete the rest of the task individually.
- Check answers as a class. Ask how much of this process they can remember while covering the chart. Ask for volunteers to share the information.

C Identifying Cause and Effect

Students complete the chart by adding the causes for the first two items and the effect for the last item. Point out that the causes and effects are portrayed vertically in this chart. You may want to complete the first item as a class.

- Allow students time to answer the questions individually.
- Have students check answers in pairs.
- Discuss as a class. Ask students whether they find it helpful to see the information presented visually in a chart. Ask students to combine each cause and effect in a sentence.

D Critical Thinking: Synthesizing

Students reflect on Reading 1, Reading 2, and the video to create a list of techniques and tips for improving memory. Encourage students to look back through the chapter for ideas.

- Allow students time to answer the questions individually.
- Have students share their answers with a partner.

- Discuss as a class. Make a list of the techniques on the board, and poll the students to find out which ones they would be most likely to use. Have the students analyze the results. Which methods are the most popular? Why?

ANSWER KEY

UNDERSTANDING THE READING

A   1; 2; 4

(Note: Option 3 is incorrect; long-term memories are stored in the neocortex. Option 5 is incorrect; the rats couldn't remember the route because they were given a drug that stopped brain-wave activity.)

B 1. hippocampus (Note: Paragraph C; this is implied, though not explicitly stated.)

2. non-REM (Note: In the flow chart, the step after this is "The brain creates sharp wave ripples ..." As mentioned in paragraph C, this occurs during the deepest level of sleep, so Non-REM Stage 3 is the correct answer here.)

3. hippocampus

4. neocortex

C   Answers will vary. Possible answers:

Causes: One group of rats was given a drug that stopped brain-wave activity; the Rutgers study.

Effects: This improves memory.

D   Answers will vary. Possible answers:

acronyms; rhymes; loci method; avoiding stress; playing games

---

Ideas for... **EXPANSION**

Have students work in pairs to write a dialog between a doctor and an English student who isn't getting enough sleep. Ask: What problems might the student have? What would the doctor's advice be? How would the doctor explain the cause-and-effect relationships?

Have students write the dialog, practice it, and then present it either to the class or in small groups.

Writing

OVERVIEW

In this section, students prepare to write a cause-and-effect paragraph about improving one's memory. The lesson starts by teaching students how to use *by* + gerund. Students then learn how to use an outline to develop their ideas. In the *Writing Task*, students apply these lessons by brainstorming, planning, and writing about memory. As added support, they will encounter two drafts of sample paragraphs and revising strategies that the author used. Students will use a checklist to revise their own paragraphs. Editing practice helps students correct common mistakes with *by* + gerund. After this, students write the final drafts of their paragraphs.

EXPLORING WRITTEN ENGLISH *(pages 95–97)*

A Noticing

Students are expected to notice how *by* + gerund is used in cause-and-effect sentences. This exercise is to be done before going over the information in the *Language for Writing* box.

- Have students complete the task individually.
- Check answers as a class. Ask students to circle the *by* + gerund in the sentences. What do they notice about the structure of the sentences?

Language for Writing: Using *By* + Gerund

The *Language for Writing* box describes how *by* + gerund is used in cause-and-effect relationships. It explains how the gerund (verb form + *-ing*) is used to describe the cause. One way to explain this is that the act of completing the action described in the verb leads to the result. Have a student read the text in the *Language for Writing* box aloud. Direct students to the examples in exercise A and in the box. Point out that when the cause comes before the effect, a comma is needed between the two clauses.

B Language for Writing

Students practice writing cause-and-effect sentences with *by* + gerund. They combine the information in two separate sentences into one. Remind students to use commas appropriately. Ask a student to read the example sentence aloud before they begin.

- Allow students time to complete the activity individually.
- Have them check answers in pairs.
- Check answers as a class.

C Language for Writing

Students create their own sentences using *by* + gerund. Before beginning the exercise, you may want to create a word web on the board with ideas about exercise and stress. Be sure to keep these ideas brief.

- Allow students time to complete the task individually.
- Have students compare answers in groups of three or four. Ask students whether they have similar or different ideas.
- Check answers as a class. Elicit example sentences from each group. Make sure that students are aware of comma placement.

Ideas for… EXPANSION

Before class, prepare enough papers for a 2:1 ratio in the class. Write an **effect** at the top of each page. Examples: *You will get a good grade in English; You can run a marathon; You will improve your finances.* Explain to students that they should write a "*by* + gerund" phrase as the **cause** at the bottom of the page. Have students form pairs, write causes, fold the paper over their answer so that the *by* + gerund clause is hidden, and then pass the paper to another pair. The new pair should not look at the previous answer; they should write their own, fold the paper again, and pass it to a new pair. Model this before students begin. After students have written answers on five or six papers, collect the papers, unfold them, and read the statements aloud to the class. Vote on the best ideas.

See Grammar Summary on page 222 of the Student Book for additional practice with Language for Writing: Using *By* + Gerund.

EXPLORING WRITTEN ENGLISH

A 1. C

2. E (Note: Remind students of ROY G BIV in exercise A on page 88.)

3. E

4. E

5. C (Note: Having *self-esteem* means that you feel good about yourself.)

6. E

LANGUAGE FOR WRITING

B 1. By getting a good night's sleep, you help your brain form long-term memories.

2. You can memorize the order of a deck of cards by using the loci method.

3. The scientists stopped the rats' brain waves by giving them a drug.

4. By making a shopping list, you can remember what items you need to buy.

C Answers will vary. Possible answers:

1. I try to relieve stress by listening to good music.

2. By meditating every morning, I start my day in a relaxed way.

3. By planning all my meals for the day in the morning, I can avoid eating junk food.

Writing Skill: Using an Outline

The *Writing Skill* box describes how using an outline can help the development of a paragraph. The *Writing Skill* box teaches students to write a topic sentence, supporting ideas, and details. The box explains that this can improve the flow of writing. It should help students determine whether they need more information, whether they have unnecessary information, and how to order their paragraphs.

• Have a student read the text in the *Writing Skill* box aloud.

• Ask students whether they use an outline in their writing. Why or why not? Elicit academic subjects in which they use outlines.

• Ask students to find the *by* + gerund clause in the *Writing Skill* box. What cause and effect are mentioned?

D Writing Skill

Students should read the outline and then match the longer sentences with the information in the outline. Direct students to the example in the book, and remind them that they can refer to the *Writing Skill* box as necessary.

• Allow students time to complete the task individually.

• Have students check answers in pairs.

• Check answers as a class.

E Writing Skill

Students should look at the two sentences from exercise D that are not related to the outline. Explain that the concluding statement will be something that is used at the conclusion, or end, of the paragraph. If something is unrelated, then it does not connect with the topic sentence.

• Have students complete the task individually.

• Check answers as a class. Elicit the reason why the statements provide a concluding statement and are unrelated to the topic.

F Writing Skill

Students should find the cause-and-effect relationships. Refer them to the *Reading Skill* box on page 88, and remind them to look for signal words.

WRITING SKILL

D   a, c, d, e, f, h, i

E   g, j, b

F   Answers will vary. Possible answers:

You can also memorize a route by creating a mental picture of it. (Note: Sentence f)

By visualizing the route, you will learn it faster. (Note: Sentence i)

Many people use driving apps nowadays, so they don't need to memorize a route. (Note: Sentence b)

40 MINS WRITING TASK *(page 98)*

A Brainstorming

Remind students that brainstorming is a useful first step for gathering ideas before writing. Read the *Goal* box aloud so students will be familiar with the writing task before brainstorming. Provide one or two example ideas. Ideas should be briefly worded. They need not be listed in any order.

• Allow time for students to complete the task individually.

• Have students share their ideas in pairs and offer feedback to each other.

B Planning

Students follow steps 1 to 3 to complete the outline. Have a student read the steps aloud. Remind students that complete sentences are not necessary for the supporting ideas and details. It is more important to focus on organizing their information.

• Allow time for students to complete their outlines individually. Provide assistance as needed.

C First Draft

Have students write first drafts of their paragraphs based on their outlines.

- Allow time for students to complete the task individually. Provide assistance as needed. Refrain from error correction at this point.

WRITING TASK

A   Answers will vary. Possible answers: stop multitasking and concentrate on one task at a time; take naps; take regular breaks from technology; meditate; try new and challenging tasks

B   Answers will vary. Possible answers:

Topic Sentence: There are many different ways to improve memory, including using the loci method, using acronyms, and getting enough sleep.

Supporting Idea 1: loci method (memory palace)

Details: USA Memory champion organizes a deck of cards

Supporting Idea 2: acronyms

Details: ROY G BIV (rainbow)

Supporting Idea 3: getting enough sleep

Details: brain-wave activity—long-term memory

REVISING PRACTICE *(page 99)*

The *Revising Practice* box contains an exercise that demonstrates several ways students can improve their first drafts.

- Allow time for students to analyze the two drafts and complete the exercise.
- Check answers as a class. Ask students to identify each change and explain how it makes the revised draft stronger.

D Revised Draft

Students should apply the revision techniques used in the *Revising Practice* box to their own drafts, where applicable.

- Explain to students that they will be using the questions as a guide for checking and improving their drafts.
- As a class, go over the questions carefully to make sure students understand them.
- Allow students time to revise their paragraphs.

EDITING PRACTICE *(page 100)*

The *Editing Practice* box trains students to spot and correct common errors related to *by* + gerund. As a class, go over the information in the box carefully.

- Allow students time to complete the exercise individually.
- Check answers in pairs.
- Check answers as a class by asking students to read their corrected sentences aloud and explain the errors.

REVISING PRACTICE

    b, a, a, d, c

EDITING PRACTICE

1. You can't remember all of the information in a lecture just by <u>listening</u> to it.
2. By taking notes while you <u>listen, you</u> can remember information better.
3. By <u>writing</u> a summary of your notes after a lecture, you will remember the information more easily.
4. By taking notes and <u>making</u> lists, you transfer information from internal to external memory. (Explanation: Both *take* and *make* should be in the gerund form. They both are part of the *by* + gerund phrase.)
5. One study shows that by getting a good night's <u>sleep, people</u> remember a skill (such as playing the piano) 30 percent better.
6. You can improve your memory by eating a healthy diet and <u>exercising</u> regularly.

E Final Draft

Have students apply the skills taught in *Editing Practice* to their own revised drafts and check for any other errors.

- Allow time for students to work individually on editing their drafts.
- Walk around and monitor students as they work. Provide assistance as needed.
- Collect their work once they have completed it.
- For the next class, show anonymous examples of good paragraphs and common errors.

🕙 10 MINS   UNIT REVIEW

Students can work in groups on this recap of the unit. For question **1**, encourage students to use the target words when appropriate. For questions **2** and **3**, encourage them to check the relevant pages of the unit for answers.

- Allow students time to answer the three questions in groups. For question **1**, ask groups whether they changed their opinions as they studied this unit.
- Ask each group to present its answer for question **1**. As a class, have students vote for what they believe is the most effective technique for memorization.

ANIMALS AND MEDICINE

6

UNIT OVERVIEW

The theme of this unit is the role of animals in medicine, including collection of toxins from snakes and frogs, the benefits and dangers of toxins, researching and rebuilding extinct viruses, and the use of chimpanzees in medical research.

- **READING 1:** A scientist, Zoltan Takacs, has a mission to catalogue different snake venoms in the hope that these may be used for medical purposes.

- **VIDEO:** The video describes the process that a scientist, Valerie Clark, uses to study insects that are the sources of a frog's toxins in Madagascar.

- **READING 2:** Chimpanzees have long been used for medical research, but with a law banning this research, chimps once used for research now live in a sanctuary. However, some scientists argue that they are still needed for medical research.

Students draw on what they've read and watched to write an argumentative paragraph. The unit prepares them by introducing vocabulary to talk about animals in medicine, identifying pros and cons, and explaining how to use language to show concessions. They also learn how to express agreement and disagreement. Lastly, students brainstorm to help them plan their paragraphs and then revise and edit their drafts.

THINK AND DISCUSS (page 101)

The questions help prepare students for the subject matter covered in the unit—animals and medicine. The scene depicts a colorful sea slug called a nudibranch.

- Discuss the photo as a class. What do students think the photo and the unit are about? Provide your own overview.

- Discuss the two questions as a class. For question **1**, if any students have been bitten or stung, have them describe the experience. For question **2**, list the animals that scientists like to use in medical research on the board. Why are these animals used? Then ask students whether they think this is ethical. Why or why not?

ANSWER KEY

THINK AND DISCUSS

1. Answers will vary. Possible answers: Yes, I was stung by a bee. It was very painful.

2. Answers will vary. Possible answers:

   mice, rats, fruit flies, primates; to determine the effects of medicines on humans without putting humans at risk

---

EXPLORE THE THEME (pages 102–103)

The opening spread features information about animals that have contributed to medicine.

- Allow students time to look at the photographs and captions, read the information, and answer the questions in part **A** individually. Elicit definitions for: *saliva* (spit) and *hormone* (a chemical in the body).

- Discuss answers as a class. Ask students to share the reasons for their answers to question **2**.

- Have students answer the question in part **B**. Remind students to use the correct forms of the words.

ANSWER KEY

EXPLORE THE THEME

A   Answers will vary. Possible answers:

1. Animals can be used to test new drugs, and they can also be a source of a new drug.

2. Many people in the world have diabetes, so I think the Gila monster's saliva is very important.

B   knowledge; possibility; side effect

Reading 1

PREPARING TO READ *(page 104)*

A Building Vocabulary

Students find the seven blue words in the passage and use contextual clues to guess the meanings. Remind students to look for the parts of speech to help them better understand the new words.

- Allow time for students to complete the exercise individually.
- Check answers as a class. Ask which words students already knew. Which ones are new to them?
- Elicit example sentences for each vocabulary item. Ask: What are some *resources* you have for learning English? What are some *concerns* you have about your future? Do you have a *specific* reason for learning English? If so, what is it?

See Vocabulary Extension 6A on page 208 of the Student Book for additional practice with Word Link: en- (meaning "putting or causing to be in a certain condition").

B Using Vocabulary

Students should practice using the new vocabulary items while answering the three questions.

- Have students discuss their answers in pairs.
- Compare answers as a class. Elicit example answers from students. For question **1**, write a list on the board. For question **2**, ask whether students have experienced these side effects. For question **3**, ask students to also name some diseases that doctors *can* cure. Remind students of unit 2, in which they learned about the invention of antibiotics.

C Brainstorming

Students discuss the question in pairs. Ideas can be brief.
- Have students work in pairs to complete the exercise.
- Discuss the question as a class. What do they think is the biggest problem that scientists face?

D Predicting

Students skim the reading passage and decide which sentence best describes Zoltan Takacs. Remind students to skim the passage quickly and not to stop at unknown words.

- Allow time for students to skim the reading and answer the question. You may want to set a time limit of 1 to 2 minutes.
- Have students check answers in pairs.
- Have students compare their answers as a class. Ask them how they arrived at their answers. Revisit this question after the reading.

ANSWER KEY

PREPARING TO READ   P. 104

A 1. target
 2. concerned
 3. disease
 4. cure
 5. specific
 6. resources
 7. endangered

B Answers will vary. Possible answers:

 1. panda bears; polar bears; rhinoceroses; orangutans

 2. headaches; drowsiness; lack of/enhanced appetite; weakness; hair loss

 3. cancer; diabetes; AIDS; Parkinson's disease; Alzheimer's disease *Viruses*

C Answers will vary. Possible answers: Scientists may have to travel to remote and dangerous places to collect samples; they might not know the language spoken in the area; they might get bitten or stung themselves.

D b

 2.01 Have students read the passage individually, or play the audio and have students read along.

OVERVIEW OF THE READING

The reading passage describes the work of Zoltan Takacs and his colleagues, who collect venom for scientific research from snakes around the world. Takacs believes that toxins can help cure many diseases. He is afraid that if species disappear, the opportunity to develop cures will disappear, too.

Online search terms: The Bite that Heals; Zoltan Takacs; National Geographic mamba

UNDERSTANDING THE READING *(page 107)*

A Understanding Main Ideas

Students are asked to match each section to the correct heading. Elicit the meanings of: *tell the difference* (differentiate, distinguish), *potentially* (possibly), and *biodiversity* (the existence of a wide variety of animal and plant species in their natural environment).

- Have students complete the activity individually.
- Have them check their answers in pairs.
- Check answers as a class. Ask students if they are surprised by what they have read. If so, what surprises them?

B Understanding Details

Students test their understanding of the details in the passage by answering questions.

- Allow students time to answer the questions individually.
- Have them form pairs and compare their answers.
- Check answers as a class. Ask students where they found the information to arrive at their answers.

C Critical Thinking: Understanding Metaphors and Similes

The *Critical Thinking* box describes two types of figurative language, metaphors and similes, which allow two things to be compared. By noticing a similarity between two things, the reader can better understand the writer's idea. Have a student read the text in the box aloud. Elicit that Sam is not actually a fish and the teeth are not actually daggers, but the author's use of this language helps the reader to imagine the meaning. You may want to discuss the first example as a class.

- Have students answer the questions individually.
- Have students check answers in pairs.
- Discuss the answers as a class. Elicit that the other answers are all *literal* meanings of the expression. Ask students whether the figurative language helps them better understand the passage. Why or why not?

D Critical Thinking: Reflecting

Have students think about what they have read and discuss their personal opinions. Remind them to justify their opinions.

- Have students discuss their answers in pairs.
- Discuss answers as a class. Take a vote to see who would like this job and who would not. Then ask volunteers from both groups to explain why they would or would not like this job.

Ideas for… EXPANSION

Have students imagine that they have the chance to interview Zoltan Takacs for a TV show. Have them work in pairs. First, ask them to decide what type of talk show they want to create (serious, funny, for children, etc.). Next, what do they want to ask him? They should create a list of three to five questions. Then they should work with a new partner to role-play the interview. One student should be Zoltan, and the other should be the interviewer. Encourage students to be as creative as possible. Afterward, ask volunteers to share the best answers to their questions.

Interview assignment
5 indirect questions

ANSWER KEY

UNDERSTANDING THE READING

A 1. b; **2.** c; **3.** a

B Answers will vary. Possible answers:

1. He wants to see if their venom can cure human diseases. (See Paragraph B.)

2. They can hit a single target, so they have fewer side effects. (See Paragraph C.)

3. Some endangered species can be sources of medicines. So if we lose a species, we could potentially lose a medicine that saves human lives. (See Paragraphs E and F.)

4. They have a molecule that "disguises" the target and stops the toxin from making contact. (See "Why Doesn't Snake Venom Affect the Snake?")

C 1. b; **2.** b; **3.** a

D Answers will vary. Possible answers: Yes, I think this would be a great job because it's exciting and you have the ability to help people all over the world. OR No, because I'm terrified of snakes!

20 MINS DEVELOPING READING SKILLS (page 108)

Reading Skill: Identifying Pros and Cons

The *Reading Skill* box describes how to identify pros and cons. Pros are positive points (advantages), and cons are negative points (disadvantages) about a topic. Noting pros and cons while reading can help students better understand a topic, evaluate a writer's argument, and form their own opinions. Have volunteers read the text in the box and the examples aloud. Ask students if they can think of any other pros or cons to add to the list.

A Identifying Pros and Cons

Have students read the title of the passage and the first footnote that explains what a *virus* is. Elicit the meaning of an *extinct virus* (one that no longer infects people). Ask students why scientists might want to make an extinct virus alive again. Do they think this is a good or bad idea? Then have students read the information and write pros and cons in the chart. Remind students that they do not have to write full sentences. You may want to offer one example to start.

- Allow time for students to complete the task individually.
- Have students check answers in pairs.
- Check answers as a class. Create the chart on the board and fill it in as a class.

B Critical Thinking: Evaluating

Students look at their lists of pros and cons in exercise **A** and form their own opinions.

- Allow students a minute to think about their opinions individually. Encourage them to write brief notes.
- Have students discuss their answers in pairs and justify their opinions.
- Discuss answers as a class. Ask volunteers to explain why they chose their answers. Have students vote on whether virologists should or should not continue to study extinct viruses. Then ask what restrictions they think should or could be placed on scientists.

groups

> ### Ideas for... EXPANSION
>
> Have students work in two large groups. One group represents virologists who want to study extinct viruses. The other group represents doctors who are worried about the possible dangers. Give students 5 to 7 minutes to prepare their arguments. Then have the virologists stand in a circle facing outward. Have the doctors stand so that each one is facing one of the virologists. Explain that they will debate their case one on one. After 1 minute, the students in the outside circle move one step clockwise, so each is speaking with another person. Repeat this, switching every 1 to 2 minutes, at least four times. Ask students if they felt their arguments improved after the fourth debate. When this exercise has been completed, have students vote on which group they agree with.

P.108

ANSWER KEY

DEVELOPING READING SKILLS

A   Answers will vary. Possible answers:

Pros: We could learn more about how viruses cause disease and how humans developed in the past. We could develop vaccines in case the extinct viruses reappear.

Cons: The scientists and the public could become infected with the virus, and there would be no cure. Our immune systems probably wouldn't have the ability to fight an extinct virus.

B   Answers will vary. Possible answers:

I don't think virologists should continue studying extinct viruses because it's just too dangerous. If just one person becomes infected, it could lead to an outbreak and many people could die.

Video

40 MINS **VIEWING: THE FROG LICKER** *(pages 109–110)*

Overview of the Video

The video describes the work of scientist Valerie Clark, who studies frogs to find information on toxins that could be valuable for medical research. The Mantella poison frog in Madagascar is particularly interesting because it has a variety of toxins that are produced from the insects the frog eats.

Online search terms: Mantella Poison Frog; Valerie Clark National Geographic; Frog Licker; Madagascar nature

BEFORE VIEWING

A Predicting

Have students look at the picture and read the caption. Have students predict why she is licking the frog.

- Have students discuss possible reasons in pairs.
- Discuss answers with the class. Write a list on the board, and revisit this question after watching the video to see whether students' predictions were correct.

B Learning about the Topic

The paragraph prepares students for the video by giving them background information on some poisonous animals. Have students read the paragraph and answer the questions.

- Have students complete the task individually.
- Have students check answers in pairs.
- Discuss answers as a class. Point out that the poison dart frog is different from the Mantella poison frog.

C Vocabulary in Context

This exercise introduces students to some of the key words used in the video. Encourage students to try to infer the meanings from the context. Remind students to use the correct word form for each word.

- Have students complete the task individually.
- Check answers as a class. Elicit example sentences for each word. Ask: What is a good *source* of vitamin C? Are there *primary forests* near where you live? What do you hope to find when you follow the *leads* in the game Cluedo?

P.109

P.110

ANSWER KEY

BEFORE VIEWING

A   Answers will vary. Possible answer: Maybe this helps her determine whether the frog is poisonous. If the frog is very small, she might not be affected by the poison.

B **1.** by biting other creatures or by releasing toxins through their skin

2. Answers will vary. Possible answer: Hunters could coat their arrows or knives with the toxin to kill large animals.

3. A poison dart frog, because although a centipede can produce venom, it is not fatal to humans.

C **1.** lead
2. source
3. primary forest

WHILE VIEWING

A ▶ Understanding Main Ideas

Have students read the items silently before you play the video. Then have the students watch the video and check which types of information Valerie Clark hopes to learn. Have them complete the task while the video is playing.

- Have students form pairs and compare answers.
- Check answers as a class. Then ask students whether their predictions for Before Viewing exercise **A** were correct.

B ▶ Understanding Details

Have students read the questions and write any answers they recall from the first viewing before playing the video a second time. Elicit the meaning of *GPS* (global positioning system—a satellite navigation system that provides precise location information).

- Have students complete the task while the video is playing.
- Have students form pairs and compare answers.
- Check answers as a class. Ask students if there are any other words that they need to have explained, and elicit definitions from volunteers.

DB #2

ANSWER KEY

WHILE VIEWING

A   2, 3

B   Wording of answers will vary. Correct answers:

1. wipe their backs with a tissue soaked in alcohol

2. It is only mildly toxic to humans.

3. Stop cutting down rain forests.

AFTER VIEWING

A Critical Thinking: Inferring Meaning

Students should discuss the quote from the video and the figurative language used, which is highlighted in bold. As an example, remind students of the beginning of the video (or show the scene) where Clark talks about *the season for love.* Elicit that this is the mating season and another example of figurative language.

- Have students discuss the quote in pairs.
- Discuss as a class. Ask students whether they have heard this expression before.

B Critical Thinking: Synthesizing

Students draw on information from Reading 1 and the video to compare the jobs of the two scientists.

- Allow students time to answer the question individually. Encourage students to make a Venn diagram in order to compare their ideas.
- Have students discuss their answer in pairs
- Discuss as a class. Draw a Venn diagram on the board and add students' answers.

ANSWER KEY

AFTER VIEWING

A   If you eat healthy food, you will be healthy; and if you eat unhealthy food, you will be unhealthy.

B   Answers will vary. Possible answers:
1. They both have difficult jobs, travel to faraway places, and have the goal of helping medical research. Zoltan's job is more dangerous because snakes are generally deadlier to humans than the frogs that Valerie works with.

Reading 2

PREPARING TO READ (page 111)

A Building Vocabulary

In this exercise, students read the definitions of the eight vocabulary words from the reading passage. Then they choose the correct word for each sentence. Remind students to use the correct forms of the words.

- Have students complete the exercise individually.
- Check answers as a class. Elicit example sentences for each vocabulary item. Ask: Are you a very *emotional* person? Why or why not? What is the *mission* of your school? (Refer to the school's mission statement, if necessary.)

See Vocabulary Extension 6B on page 208 of the Student Book for additional practice with Word Web: Adjectives for Emotion.

B Using Vocabulary

Students should use the new vocabulary items while discussing the two questions.

- Have students work in pairs to answer the questions.
- Discuss answers as a class. Elicit example answers from students. Ask students whether they can describe any experiments they have conducted.

C Brainstorming

Students brainstorm ways that chimpanzees and other apes have been used in research. Make sure that students know what chimpanzees and apes are. Direct their attention to the photograph on page 112, if necessary.

- Have students discuss their ideas in pairs.
- Have students share their ideas with the class. Ask if they have heard about any specific studies. Then ask what they think the pros and cons of using apes in medical research could be.

ANSWER KEY

PREPARING TO READ

A 1. mission
   2. procedures
   3. conduct
   4. experiments; laboratories
   5. invasive
   6. advances
   7. emotional

B Answers will vary. Possible answers:

   1. I have conducted physics experiments, such as creating a model volcano. I like conducting these kinds of scientific experiments because we get to watch the effects of the experiment occur in front of us.

   2. Some important advances in medicine include organ transplants and treatments for diabetes.

C Answers will vary. Possible answers:

   Chimpanzees have been used to learn more about HIV and hepatitis. They were injected with the viruses so that scientists could learn more about the effects of the viruses and how to cure disease.

 2.02 Have students read the passage individually, or play the audio and have students read along.

OVERVIEW OF THE READING

The reading passage describes the use of chimpanzees for medical research. Because of a new law protecting chimpanzees from medical experiments, a new sanctuary (Chimp Haven) has opened, where chimpanzees can live together. However, some scientists argue that the use of chimpanzees in medical research benefits both humans and wild chimpanzees.

Online search terms: Chimp Haven; Jane Goodall TED Talk; Steven Wise TED Talk; chimpanzee medical research

UNDERSTANDING THE READING (page 114)

A Understanding the Main Idea

Students read the passage and then choose the best summary from three options.

- Allow time for students to complete the task individually.
- Check answers as a class. Ask students to explain why the other options are incorrect.

B Understanding Details

Students read the statements and decide which ones are true, false, or *not given*. Explain that NG (*not given*) means that the answer is not found in the text. If some students finish early, have them correct the false statements.

- Allow time for students to complete the task individually.
- Have students check answers in pairs.
- Check answers as a class. Ask students to correct the false statements.

C Understanding Pronoun References

Students read the sentences. Elicit what pronouns are and why it is important to understand what they represent. Elicit that the information will almost always come *before* the pronoun.

- Allow students time to answer the questions individually.
- Have students check answers in pairs.
- Check answers with the class. If possible, write the sentences on the board, and draw an arrow from the pronoun to the subject in each.

D Identifying Pros and Cons

Students complete the chart with pros and cons, based on the material in the reading passage.

- Allow students time to complete the chart individually.
- Have students compare answers in groups of three.
- Discuss as a class. On the board, create a T-chart with pros and cons. As students share their answers, write them on the board.

E Critical Thinking: Evaluating

Students look at their lists of pros and cons in exercise **D** and form their own opinions.

- Have students read the question, assess the chart in exercise **D**, and decide whether the advantages outweigh the disadvantages.
- Allow time for students to discuss their opinions in pairs. Encourage students to justify their opinions.
- Discuss answers as a class. Have a class vote.

group groups

ANSWER KEY

UNDERSTANDING THE READING

A c

B 1. F (See Paragraph B.)
2. F (See Paragraph C.)
3. NG (Explanation: Paragraph C states that many lab chimps were intentionally given HIV and hepatitis viruses, but there is no mention in the reading passage of malaria or cancer.)
4. T (See Paragraphs C and E.)
5. NG
6. T (See Paragraph I.)

C 1. c
2. b

D Answers will vary. Possible answers:

Pros: can advance human health and medical research; help to find vaccines for humans; help to find cures for diseases that affect chimps, such as an Ebola vaccine for wild chimps

Cons: Chimps in the wild are captured and sold for research, leading to reduced populations in the wild; chimps live solitary lives, don't get to go outside, and live in small cages; are infected with diseases; chimps are intelligent and emotional creatures, like humans, so they can feel pain and loneliness.

E Answers will vary. Possible answer: No, I don't think scientists should continue using chimps in medical research because chimps are intelligent and have feelings similar to those of humans. It is cruel to give chimpanzees diseases that will make them suffer.

Ideas for… EXPANSION

If computers are available, have students go to the Chimp Haven website, where there is a section called *Meet the Chimps*. Have students work individually or in pairs to click on different chimpanzees and read about them. Have each student choose a chimp, read about it, and add some adjectives to describe that chimp's personality. Then have students introduce their chimps to the class. Make sure that students can show the images of their chimps to the class.

Writing

OVERVIEW

In this section, students prepare to write an argumentative paragraph about using animals in medical research. The lesson starts by teaching students how to make concessions in writing (show two sides of a situation in one sentence). Students then learn how to express agreement and disagreement. In the *Writing Task*, students apply these lessons by brainstorming, planning, and writing their opinions. As added support, they will encounter two drafts of sample paragraphs and revising strategies that the author used. Students will use a checklist to revise their own paragraphs. Editing practice helps students correct common mistakes with concessions. After this, students write the final drafts of their paragraphs.

EXPLORING WRITTEN ENGLISH *(pages 115–117)*

A Noticing

Students are expected to notice how concessions are used by reading the information and determining which argument the author feels is more important. This exercise is to be done before going over the information in the *Language for Writing* box. If students feel this exercise is confusing, reassure them that they will learn more about it later.

- Have students complete the task individually.
- Have students check their answers in pairs.
- Check answers as a class. Ask students whether they notice what each of the more important sections has in common (and what each of the less important sections has in common).

Language for Writing: Making Concessions

The *Language for Writing* box describes how to make concessions. It explains that clauses beginning with *although* or *even though* are concession clauses; this information is true, but not as strong as the information in the main clause. Have students read the text in the *Language for Writing* box aloud. Have students look again at exercise **A** and rewrite the sentences, switching around the two clauses and making changes, including comma changes where necessary. Remind students that each clause needs a subject and a verb! Allow time for students to write the sentences. Then write them on the board.

B Language for Writing

Students practice writing sentences making concessions. They should read the two items of information and then connect these in one sentence to reflect the information. Have a student read the example aloud. Elicit that the writer has used a pronoun in the second clause and has connected the clauses with a comma.

- Allow students time to complete the activity individually.
- Have them check answers in pairs.
- Check answers as a class. Have volunteers write the sentences on the board. Ask: If the information in the two clauses were reversed, how would it change the message?

C Language for Writing

Students create their own sentences in which they make concessions. Before beginning the exercise, remind students that they can write about any topic they choose. You may want to offer an example to start. Write an example sentence on the board, and label the "more important" and "less important" sections.

- Allow students time to complete the task individually.
- Have students read their sentences aloud in groups of three or four. Have each group check the grammar and then choose two sentences to write on the board.
- Compare the sentences on the board as a class. Correct any that contain errors.

Ideas for... EXPANSION

Have students write stories using concessions. Have students work in pairs, and begin the story with the following two sentences: "As I was walking to school, I saw a _____. Even though _____, I _____."

Allow students time to think of imaginative ideas. Then collect the papers and give them to different pairs. Have the next pair read the beginning of the story and write another concession sentence, continuing the story. Continue switching papers three or four more times. At the fifth switch, have each pair read the story they are given and correct the grammar and spelling. Then have them write a concluding sentence. Post the stories around the classroom for students to read, or have volunteers read their stories aloud.

ANSWER KEY

EXPLORING WRITTEN ENGLISH

A **1.** b (<u>Even though</u>)

2. b (<u>Although</u>)

3. a (<u>even though</u>)

4. b (<u>Even though</u>)

LANGUAGE FOR WRITING

B **1.** Although a small amount of arsenic can be deadly, it is still used to treat certain diseases.

2. The poison dart frog is highly toxic even though it is just two inches long.

3. Even though chimpanzee experimentation can lead to advances in human health, invasive research on chimps has been largely banned.

C Answers will vary. Possible answers:

1. Although he used chimpanzees in medical research, he always treated them well.

2. I did all my homework even though I wasn't feeling well.

Writing Skill: Writing an Argumentative Paragraph

The *Writing Skill* box describes the steps needed to convince a reader that your point of view is valid, and points out the importance of expressing both agreement and disagreement in an argumentative paragraph. The *Writing Skill* box teaches students to state the issue, the argument, and then the reasons why an argument is valid. The box lists phrases for agreement and disagreement. Have students read the text in the *Writing Skill* box aloud. Ask students which of these phrases they already use, and which one sounds the most formal.

D Writing Skill

Students read the paragraph and underline the three sentences that make a concession. Remind students to look for the words *even though* or *although*.

• Allow students time to complete the task individually.

• Have students check answers in pairs

• Check answers as a class.

E Writing Skill

Students read the paragraph again and answer the questions.

• Have students complete the task individually.

• Have students check their answers in pairs.

• Check answers as a class.

ANSWER KEY

WRITING SKILL

D **1.** First, although zoos … and habits.

2. In addition, although keeping … the wild.

3. Finally, even though zoos … enforced.

E Answers will vary. Possible answers:

Main Argument: It is wrong to keep animals in zoos.

Supporting Idea 1: Living in zoos negatively affects animals' routines and habits.

Concession: Zoos allow people to see animals that they wouldn't otherwise see.

Details: Lions in zoos aren't able to hunt for food in their natural habitats and get aggressive.

Supporting Idea 2: Zoos don't increase endangered animal populations in the wild.

Concession: Keeping animals in zoos helps protect endangered animals.

Details: Animals born in zoos usually stay in zoos their whole lives.

Supporting Idea 3: Animal welfare standards aren't always enforced.

Concession: Zoos are supposed to meet minimum requirements for animal welfare by law.

Details: Zebras at a Washington zoo died because of insufficient food.

 WRITING TASK *(page 118)*

A Brainstorming

Read the text in the *Goal* box aloud so students will be familiar with the writing task. Ideas should be briefly worded. They need not be listed in any order.

• Allow time for students to complete their charts individually. Provide assistance as needed.

• Have students share their ideas in pairs and offer feedback to each other.

B Planning

Students follow steps 1 to 3 to complete their outlines. Have a student read the steps aloud. Remind students that complete sentences are not necessary for the supporting ideas, concessions, and details. It is more important to focus on organizing their information.

• Allow time for students to complete their outlines individually. Provide assistance as needed.

C First Draft

Have students write first drafts of their paragraphs based on their outlines.
- Allow time for students to complete the task individually. Provide assistance as needed. Refrain from error correction at this point.

ANSWER KEY

WRITING TASK

A Answers will vary. Possible answers:

Pros: Medicines made from animal venom have fewer side effects; some medical advances can help animals in the wild, too.

Cons: cruel to the animals; medicines may affect humans and animals differently.

B Answers will vary. Possible answers:

Main Argument: Scientists should not be allowed to use animals for medical research because it is cruel and unnecessary.

Supporting Idea 1: Animals are often harmed.

Concession: Scientists don't want to be cruel.

Details: Animals live in small cages; may be injured or in pain during testing.

Supporting Idea 2: Drugs don't always have the same effect on animals and humans.

Concession: Experiments with animals can lead to advances in human health.

Details: Some drugs are safe for animals but not for humans.

REVISING PRACTICE *(page 119)*

The *Revising Practice* box contains an exercise that demonstrates several ways students can improve their first drafts.
- Allow time for students to analyze the two drafts and complete the exercise.
- Check answers as a class.

D Revised Draft

Students apply the revision techniques used in the *Revising Practice* box to their own drafts.
- Explain to students that they will be using the questions as a guide for improving their drafts.
- As a class, go over the questions carefully to make sure students understand them.
- Allow students time to revise their paragraphs.

EDITING PRACTICE *(page 120)*

The *Editing Practice* box trains students to spot and correct common errors related to making concessions. As a class, go over the information in the box carefully.
- Allow students time to complete the exercise individually.
- Check answers as a class by asking students to read their corrected sentences aloud and explain the errors.

ANSWER KEY

REVISING PRACTICE

d, a, b, c

EDITING PRACTICE

1. Even though she's afraid of <u>snakes, she</u> wants to study snake venoms.
2. Although the golden poison dart frog is very small, it <u>is</u> very deadly.
3. Even though the NIH is retiring its research chimpanzees, <u>it</u> will continue to use other animals for medical research.
4. Although there are potentially millions of toxins in the <u>wild, scientists</u> have studied only a couple thousand.
5. Even though black widow spider bites can be deadly to small children, <u>they</u> are not usually strong enough to kill an adult human.

E Final Draft

Have students apply the skills taught in *Editing Practice* to their own revised drafts and check for any other errors.
- Allow time for students to work individually on editing their drafts.
- Walk around and monitor students as they work. Provide assistance as needed.

10 MINS UNIT REVIEW

Students can work in groups on this recap of the unit. For question **1**, encourage students to use the target words when appropriate. For questions **2** and **3**, encourage them to check the relevant pages of the unit for answers.
- Allow students time to answer the three questions in groups.
- As a class, have students share their answers to question **1**.

NATURE'S FURY

7

UNIT OVERVIEW

The theme of this unit is extreme natural events. The unit discusses tornadoes, lightning, and wildfires.

- **READING 1:** This reading passage describes the events of April 2011, when violent tornadoes hit the southern United States. It discusses different theories about the conditions that led to this "perfect storm."

- **VIDEO:** About the causes of lightning, how it's formed, its effects, where it strikes, and how to protect yourself.

- **READING 2:** This reading is about wildfires: how, where, and why they occur. It also discusses preventive measures that can be taken. There is also a section on how firefighters fight fires.

Students draw on what they've read and watched to write a paragraph describing a natural process. The unit prepares them by introducing vocabulary to talk about natural disasters and explaining how to identify the order, or sequence, in a process. Next, language to talk about a process (using sequencing words and the simple present tense) is reviewed, and tips for evaluating sources of information are offered. Lastly, students practice brainstorming and using an outline to prepare drafts—skills that students will use in every unit's *Writing Task*.

THINK AND DISCUSS *(page 121)* — 5 MINS

The photograph shows lightning striking a hillside. The title, "Nature's Fury," and the caption narrow this down by mentioning the town of Barr, France, specifically.
- Have students study the picture, title, and captions.
- Discuss the photo as a class. Ask students: What adjectives would you use to describe this scene? Have you ever seen lightning strike? Where were you?

- Discuss the two questions as a class. For question **1**, create a word web on the board with the words *extreme natural events* in the middle. For question **2**, have the class vote on which events on the board are the top three most dangerous events. Have students explain their reasons to the class.

ANSWER KEY

THINK AND DISCUSS

Answers will vary. Possible answers:

1. tornadoes, tsunamis, earthquakes, hurricanes, blizzards, floods, volcanic eruptions
2. I think that the tsunami is the most dangerous because it can affect a very large area.

EXPLORE THE THEME *(pages 122–123)* — 15 MINS

The opening spread features a photograph of a tornado over farmland and a photograph of a firefighter fighting a wildfire in California. It also has descriptions of three extreme events in nature: lightning, tornadoes, and wildfires.
- Before students answer the questions, ask them to look at the pictures to predict what events will be mentioned.
- Allow time for students to read the information and answer the questions individually.
- Have students check answers in pairs.
- Discuss answers as a class. For question **1**, ask students if wildfires, tornadoes, or lightning are common where they live. What are some of the causes of wildfires?
- Elicit example sentences from students for each of the blue words.

ANSWER KEY

EXPLORE THE THEME

A 1. natural causes: lightning, tornadoes
   human activity: wildfires
   2. Thunderstorms can trigger tornadoes. (Note: The phrase *are born from* means that something starts from this source.) Also, lightning can start a wildfire. Wildfires can create their own weather system.

B occur; strike; violent

Reading 1

PREPARING TO READ *(page 124)*

A Building Vocabulary

The seven words in the box are key vocabulary items that appear in the passage. Students should use contextual clues to deduce the meanings of the words and complete the definitions.

- Have students complete the exercise individually.
- Check answers as a class.
- Elicit example sentences for each vocabulary item. Ask: What are two items that often collide? What is the hottest temperature on record in your region? How long does it take to get to the coast from where you live?

See Vocabulary Extension 7A on page 209 of the Student Book for additional practice with Word Link: ex- (meaning "away from")

B Using Vocabulary

Students should practice using the new vocabulary items while answering the three questions. Encourage students to try to include additional words from the blue box in their answers.

- Have students work in pairs to answer the questions.
- Check answers as a class. Elicit example answers from students. For question **1**, ask students what countries have the hottest/wettest/coldest/driest climates. For question **2**, ask whether they have experienced any of these extreme events. For question **3**, choose one recent example and elicit details from the class.

C Brainstorming

Students should practice brainstorming about the topic. If available, show video clips or photographs of tornadoes and their devastating effects.

- Have students work individually to think of answers
- Have students compare their answers in pairs.
- Check answers as a class. Elicit example answers from students and write a list on the board. After reading, revisit this list to see if any were mentioned in the reading.

D Predicting

Students scan the first paragraph to find specific information and then make a prediction about this reading.

- Have students scan the material. Give a time limit of 1 to 2 minutes.
- Have students check their answers in pairs.

- Discuss the most probable answer to part 2 as a class. Ask students how they arrived at this answer.

ANSWER KEY

PREPARING TO READ

A 1. Data (Note: *Data* is a plural noun. The singular, *datum*, is rarely used.)

   2. collide

   3. Climate

   4. coast

   5. condition

   6. on record (Note: *Record* can be a verb or a noun. You *record* information in order to have a *record* of it; this helps you to remember the information.)

   7. extends

B Answers will vary. Possible answers:

   1. hot and humid in the summer, cold in the winter

   2. blizzards and hurricanes

   3. wildfires in California; caused by a cigarette thrown out the window

C Answers will vary. Possible answers: houses are destroyed; animals and people are killed; trees fall on roads

D April 25–28, 2011; Mississippi, Alabama, Tennessee, and Georgia

   b

 2.03 Have students read the passage individually, or play the audio and have students read along.

OVERVIEW OF THE READING

The reading passage presents the history of a series of large tornadoes that struck the United States in 2011. It also discusses some of the causes and effects of tornadoes.

Online search terms: Tim Samaras; tornado alley; James Spann Ted-Ed

UNDERSTANDING THE READING *(page 127)*

A Understanding Main Ideas

Students are asked to identify the purpose for each paragraph in the reading passage. Elicit the meaning of *preventive measures*. Ask students what preventive measures can be taken to help people before a natural event occurs.

- Allow students time to complete the activity individually.
- Check answers as a class. Ask how students arrived at their answers. Elicit the meaning of "perfect storm."

B Understanding Cause and Effect

Students test their understanding of the details in the passage by completing the diagram with causes and effects. Draw the diagram on the board, and show that the arrows lead from causes to effects. Elicit the first answer (global warming) as an example.

- Allow students time to complete the diagram individually.
- Have them check their answers in pairs.
- Discuss answers as a class. Complete the diagram on the board.

C Critical Thinking: Evaluating Sources

The *Critical Thinking* box explains how to evaluate a source (the person who has given the information) by looking at his/her credentials (job, education, experience, etc.). Have a student read the text in the box aloud. Elicit *why* it is important to know a person's credentials. Why are credentials important in the digital age?

- Have students complete the task individually.
- Have students compare their answers in pairs.
- Discuss answers as a class. Ask students which theory they think is the most credible. Why? Ask students how they arrived at their choices.

D Interpreting Maps

Students look at the map connected to the reading and interpret the data. Ask students whether they are surprised by this information or if it reflects what they already know.

- Have students discuss their answers in pairs.
- Discuss answers as a class. Ask students if they have any theories for why tornadoes occur in these areas.

Ideas for... EXPANSION

Ask students whether they have seen any movies with tornadoes. If available, show students a clip of the tornado in *The Wizard of Oz,* an iconic American movie. Ask what they think happens next. Then show them a clip from the tornado scene in the movie *Twister.* Ask how the two depictions of tornadoes are similar. How are they different? If possible, have students watch one of the movies for homework and then report on it in the following class.

DEVELOPING READING SKILLS *(page 128)*

Reading Skill: Identifying Sequence

The *Reading Skill* box explains how writers use sequencing words to describe a process. Have volunteers read sections of the *Reading Skill* box aloud. Point out the difference between linking words such as *first* and *next* that introduce a sentence, and conjunctions such as *before* and *after* that join clauses together. As a class, create a word web on the board with clue words and time clauses.

A Understanding a Process

Students should look at the illustrations and fill in the blanks with the words in the box. Draw their attention to the key. Elicit the meaning of the blue and red arrows. Elicit the answer for the first question (air).

- Allow time for students to complete the task individually.
- Check answers in pairs.
- Discuss answers as a class. Ask volunteers to explain how they arrived at their answers.

B Identifying Sequence

Students should use the information in exercise A for the content of their paragraphs. They should refer to the *Reading Skill* box to use sequencing words correctly in their paragraph.

- Allow time for students to complete the task individually.
- Have students read their paragraphs aloud to a partner. Have them compare their paragraphs.
- Discuss answers as a class. Ask for two volunteers to read their paragraphs aloud. Have students notice the sequencing words used.

Ideas for… EXPANSION

Ask students to describe the process that they go through to get from the school to a nearby location (store, coffee shop, bank). Have students work in pairs to first draw three illustrations, and then write a paragraph using sequencing words, second- person present tense, and imperatives. Have them share their illustrations and paragraphs with the class.

ANSWER KEY

DEVELOPING READING SKILLS

A 1. air
2. spin
3. Warm
4. cold
5. air
6. ground

B Answers will vary. Possible answer: There are a number of steps that lead to the formation of a twister. First, winds of warm and cold air collide and begin to spin. Next, warm air rises and cold air moves downward, forming a vertical column. Finally, the spinning column of air forms a funnel cloud, which becomes a tornado when it reaches the ground.

Video

⏱ **VIEWING: LIGHTNING** *(pages 129-130)*

Overview of the Video

The video describes how lightning is formed and gives facts about where and when it occurs most frequently. It also talks about how to protect yourself in the event of lightning.

Online search terms: birth of a lightning bolt; Catumbo lightning; USA Today 4th of July Lightning

BEFORE VIEWING

A Predicting

Students should read the sentences and guess whether they are true or false. Ask: How much do you know about lightning? Assure students that they are not expected to know the answers; after watching, they will learn the answers. Explain that *on average* means that this is typically true.

- Have students complete the task individually.
- Take a class vote for each statement, and tally votes for each question on the board. Do not give the correct answers. Revisit these questions after watching the video.

B Learning About the Topic

The paragraph prepares students for the video by giving them background information about lightning. Explain that the answer to question **2** is not in the paragraph. They will need to *infer* the answer.

- Have students complete the task individually.
- Discuss answers as a class. Elicit example answers. For question **1**, ask: What does the photograph on this page show? For question **2**, write possible reasons on the board. Leave these on the board, and revisit them after watching the video.

C Vocabulary in Context

This exercise introduces students to some of the key words used in the video. Remind students to use the correct word forms. Explain that a *drought* is a period with no rain, so everything is very dry.

- Have students complete the task individually.
- Check answers as a class. Ask students to read the sentences aloud and to listen for these words in the video.

BEFORE VIEWING

A   Answers will vary. Correct answers:

1. T

2. F (50 to 100 times a second)

3. F (Most lightning strikes occur in Central Africa, the Himalayas, and South America.)

4. T

B **1.** It can melt and become a fulgurite (a tube-shaped rock).

2. Answers will vary. Possible answer: because it's in the summer and a lot of people are outdoors; because fireworks are loud, they might not notice lightning and thunder until it's too late.

C **1.** expand

2. volt

3. particle (The word *matter* refers to any physical substance.)

4. charge

WHILE VIEWING

A ▶ Understanding Main Ideas

Have students read the items silently before you play the video.

- Have them complete the task while the video is playing.
- Check the answers as a class. Ask what students can remember about each of the topics mentioned.

B ▶ Understanding Details

Have students read the paragraph and circle the words that they recall from the first viewing before playing the video a second time.

- Have students complete the task while the video is playing.
- Check answers as a class. Ask volunteers to read the sentences aloud. If students have difficulty, play sections of the video again.

WHILE VIEWING

A   1, 2, 4

B **1.** South America

2. positively; negatively

3. expanding air

4. getting in a car

AFTER VIEWING

A Reacting to the Video

Students are asked to reflect on the information in the video and correct their answers to the True/False questions in Exercise A of Before Viewing.

- Have students correct their answers individually.
- Have students check their answers in pairs.
- Check answers as a class. Ask students which answers surprised them and why.

B Critical Thinking: Synthesizing

Students are asked to reflect on the information in Reading 1 and the video. Remind them to look at the map on page 126 to find support for their answers. If necessary, play the beginning of the video, where the regions with the most lightning strikes are mentioned. If a computer is available, search online for a map of places often struck by lightning, and show this to the class.

- Have students discuss their answers in pairs.
- Discuss as a class. Ask if anyone has had a personal experience with lightning. What happened?

> **Ideas for… EXPANSION**
>
> Benjamin Franklin invented the lightning rod (he called it *the Franklin rod*) as a way to protect buildings from being damaged by lightning. He also started the first fire brigade in the United States. Tell the class about Benjamin Franklin. Then in groups of three to five, have students discuss what other invention could help protect people from a severe natural event. Have each group either research or invent a product to help minimize the effects of a natural disaster. Have each group write a short summary, and then present their ideas to the class. Encourage students to use vocabulary about inventions (unit 2). For each presentation, have the class guess whether the invention is real or the group's own idea.

AFTER VIEWING

A   See answers in *Before Viewing, exercise* A. Answers will vary. Possible answer: I was surprised that so many people die after being struck by lightning!

B **1.** the Himalayas and South America

2. Answers will vary. Possible answers: Southeast Asia, central and western parts of Australia, Antarctica

Reading 2

30 MINS

PREPARING TO READ *(page 131)*

A Building Vocabulary

In this exercise, students complete sentences that follow the same topic as the reading passage. Explain that the sentences in the box define the blue words. Remind students to use the correct forms of the words. They should use each word only once.

- Allow time for students to complete the exercise individually.
- Have students check their answers in pairs.
- Check answers as a class. Elicit example sentences for each vocabulary item. Ask: What fuel do you use to heat your homes? What can block a road? What do you particularly like about English class? What is one significant difference between lightning and tornadoes?

See Vocabulary Extension 7B on page 209 of the Student Book for additional practice with Word Forms: Changing Adjectives into Adverbs.

B Using Vocabulary

Students should use the new vocabulary items while discussing the two questions.

- Have students work in pairs to answer the questions.
- Discuss answers as a class. Elicit example answers from students. For question **1**, ask: What precautions are in place to prevent fires in your area? For question **2**, ask students whether there are safety measures in their areas to make buildings safer. If so, what are they? If not, what safety measures should be added?

C Predicting

This exercise gets students thinking about the topic. They should predict the topic based on the illustrations.

- Allow time for students to answer the question individually.
- Have students form pairs and compare their answers.
- Ask for volunteers to share their answers with the rest of the class.

ANSWER KEY

PREPARING TO READ

A 1. Frequent; threaten
2. particularly
3. on purpose
4. appropriate
5. block
6. fuel; significant (Note: In this context, *consuming* means destroying.)

B Answers will vary. Possible answers:
1. Unfortunately, fires occur quite frequently in my community. This is because there are a lot of trees and wooded areas near where I live, and they catch fire quite easily, especially during the summer.
2. remain calm; look for the exits; leave quickly; help others; alert others; check whether the door is hot before opening it

C b (Explanation: The illustration shows people trying to put out a wildfire. Both options a and c are mentioned in the passage, but the main idea is option b.)

 **2.04** Have students read the passage individually, or play the audio and have students read along.

OVERVIEW OF THE READING

The reading passage is about wildfires—how they form and the measures taken to stop them. Some measures include building fire-resistant homes, clearing land, and digging "fire lines," which are trenches around the fire.

Online search terms: wildfires National Geographic; Smokey Bear; forest firefighters

40 MINS

UNDERSTANDING THE READING *(page 134)*

A Understanding Main Ideas

Students choose the sentence that matches the paragraph to its purpose.

- Have students complete the task individually.
- Have students check answers in pairs.
- Check answers as a class. Ask students if wildfires are a problem where they live. Have they heard of any wildfires in the news? Where did these take place?

B Understanding Details

Students fill in the chart with information from the text. Explain that a *factor* is something that contributes to a result. Explain that factors will be more general than the examples.

- Allow time for students to complete the task individually.
- Have students check answers in pairs.
- Check answers as a class. Ask students where they found the answers in the reading.

C Understanding a Process

Have students read the sentences and decide whether they are true or false. Ask students who finish early to correct the false statements. The students should use the information on page 133 to answer these questions.

- Allow time for students to complete the rest of the task individually.
- Have students check answers in pairs.
- Check answers as a class. Have students correct the false statements.

D Critical Thinking: Evaluating Sources

Have students read paragraph D again and then discuss their answers in pairs. Refer them to the *Critical Thinking* box on page 127 for a reminder about credible sources.

- Have students discuss their answers with a partner.
- Discuss as a class. Ask students to justify their opinions for question **3.**

E Critical Thinking: Evaluating Sources

Have students reflect on what they have learned in this unit and choose who they would include as an additional source, noting their reason.

- Have students share their ideas with a partner. Ask whether they agree or disagree with each other.
- Discuss as a class. Elicit example answers.

Ideas for… EXPANSION

If computers are available, have students search for a news article about a recent wildfire, tornado, or lightning storm. Then have students discuss these questions in pairs:

- What happened?
- Were any preventive measures taken?
- What were the factors that led to the event?
- What sources were used in the article? Were these credible sources? Why or why not?

Have volunteers share their information with the class.

UNDERSTANDING THE READING

A **1.** c

 2. a

 3. d

 4. b

B **Factor:** weather; type of fuel

 Examples: fire moves faster uphill, southern slopes are sunnier and drier; strong winds and changes in wind direction (See Paragraph C.)

C **1.** T

 2. F (They drop fire retardant on the fire.)

 3. T

 4. F (They backburn the area between the fire line and the fire.)

D **1.** Jack Cohen is a fire researcher. He has studied wildfires for more than two decades and is an expert on how houses catch fire.

 2. that people who live in areas where wildfires frequently occur should build fire-resistant homes

 3. Answers will vary. Possible answers: I'd give him a rating of 3 because he has studied wildfires for a very long time (more than 20 years).

 4. his educational background, where he works

E Answers will vary. Possible answers:

 I would include an experienced pilot of a firefighting plane because this person may be able to provide additional information for the *Fighting Fire* section; I would include a scientist who has studied fire ecology for 30 years because this person has studied the topic widely and may be able to contribute valuable and useful information on the subject.

Writing

OVERVIEW

In this section, students prepare to write a paragraph describing a natural process. The lesson starts by teaching students language for describing a process, including the use of sequencing words and the simple present tense. Students then learn how to organize a process paragraph. In the *Writing Task*, students apply these lessons by brainstorming, planning, and writing about a process. As added support, they will encounter two drafts of sample paragraphs and revising strategies that the author used. Students will use a checklist to revise their own paragraph. Editing practice helps students use the simple present tense to explain how something happens, and to check for subject-verb agreement. After this, students write the final drafts of their paragraphs.

EXPLORING WRITTEN ENGLISH *(pages 135–137)*

A Noticing

Students are expected to notice the verbs that are used to describe a natural cycle. This exercise is to be done before going over the information in the *Language for Writing* box.

- Allow time for students to complete the task individually.
- Check answers as a class. Ask *why* they think these are all in the simple present tense. Explain that the *Language for Writing* box will give more details.

Language for Writing: Describing a Process

The *Language for Writing* box reviews the use of simple present tense for describing a process.

- Have volunteers read the information in the box aloud.
- Have students read the sentences aloud. Ask: What process do these sentences describe?
- Have students circle the subjects in the sentences in the box and in exercise A to show the subject-verb agreement.

B Language for Writing

Students practice using the information in the box by completing the sentences about the formation of snow.

- Allow students time to complete the activity individually.
- Have them check answers in pairs.
- Check answers as a class.

C Language for Writing

Students write sentences about one of the natural events described in this unit. Refer students to the *Language for Writing* box for help writing these sentences. Encourage students to try to write sentences without referring to the video and reading passages. After 2 to 3 minutes, allow them to use their books to check their answers.

- Allow students time to complete the task individually.
- Have students form pairs and compare their answers.
- Check answers as a class. Elicit example sentences about each of the three events. Check for subject-verb agreement.

ANSWER KEY

EXPLORING WRITTEN ENGLISH

A 1. raises
   2. heats; turns
   3. rises
   4. rises; gets; turns; form
   5. get; falls
   6. continues
      simple present tense

LANGUAGE FOR WRITING

B 1. is; freezes; turns
   2. collide; stick; form
   3. starts; grows
   4. become; fall
   5. falls; melts; stays

C   Answers will vary. Possible answers:
   1. Wildfires begin with a heat source.
   2. Humans cause most wildfires.
   3. Tornadoes occur when warm, wet air collides with cold, dry air.

Writing Skill: Organizing a Process Paragraph

The *Writing Skill* box is about planning a process paragraph. Explain that the sequence words and phrases indicate the order of steps or events in a process. Point out that students should include details, as well as steps, in their paragraphs.

- Ask volunteers to read the information in the box aloud.
- Have students read the steps that begin with the words in bold. Ask what process this describes. Have students circle the markers in exercise B and ask *why* writers use different markers (to make the information clear and interesting).

D Writing Skill

Students read the sentences and underline the transition words. Then they order the stages.

- Allow students time to complete the task individually.
- Check answers in pairs.
- Check answers as a class. Ask which signal words helped them make their decisions. Write the signal words on the board.

E Writing Skill

Students use the sentences in exercise **D** again to create a paragraph about the stages of a wildfire, and refer to the *Writing Skill* box for other sequence words or phrases.

- Allow students time to complete the task individually.
- Check answers as a class. Ask a volunteer to read their paragraph aloud.

WRITING TASK *(page 138)*

40 MINS

A Taking Notes

Have students make a list of natural or biological processes. Encourage students to look online, if computers are available.

- Allow students time to write ideas individually.
- Have students compare their lists in pairs and explain the processes to a partner.
- Discuss answers as a class. Write a class list of ideas on the board.

B Planning

Read the *Goal* box aloud so students will be familiar with the writing task before planning. If possible, have students research information on a natural cycle that they would like to write about. Remind students that complete sentences are not necessary. It is more important to focus on organizing their information.

- Allow time for students to complete their outlines individually. Provide assistance as needed.

C First Draft

Have students write first drafts of their paragraphs based on their outlines.

- Allow time for students to complete the task individually. Provide assistance as needed. Refrain from error correction at this point.

REVISING PRACTICE *(page 139)*

The *Revising Practice* box contains an exercise that demonstrates several ways students can improve their first drafts.

- Allow time for students to analyze the two drafts and complete the exercise.
- Check answers as a class. Ask students to identify each change and explain how it makes the revised draft stronger.

D Revised Draft

Students should apply the revision techniques used in the *Revising Practice* box to their own drafts, where applicable.

- Explain to students that they will be using the questions as a guide for checking and improving their drafts.
- As a class, go over the questions carefully to make sure students understand them.
- Allow students time to revise their paragraphs.

EDITING PRACTICE *(page 140)*

The *Editing Practice* box trains students to spot and correct common errors related to the simple present tense and subject-verb agreement. As a class, go over the information in the box carefully to make sure students understand what to look out for.

- Allow students time to complete the exercise individually.
- Check answers as a class by asking students to read their corrected sentences aloud and explain the errors.

ANSWER KEY

REVISING PRACTICE

c, b, a, b, d

EDITING PRACTICE

1. Tornadoes occur when warm, wet air <u>collides</u> with cold, dry air.
2. The rapid expansion of the air surrounding the path of a lightning bolt <u>causes</u> the sound of thunder.
3. When lightning hits a tree, the moisture inside the tree turns into gas and <u>causes</u> the tree to expand and blow up.
4. A wildfire <u>needs</u> three conditions: fuel, oxygen, and a heat source.
5. Water <u>takes</u> three forms: solid (ice), liquid, and gas (vapor).
6. When tiny ice crystals in a cloud <u>collide</u>, they form snowflakes.

E Final Draft

Have students apply the skills taught in *Editing Practice* to their own revised drafts, and check for any other errors.

- Allow time for students to work individually on editing their drafts.
- Walk around and monitor students as they work. Provide assistance as needed.
- Collect their work once they have completed it.
- For the next class, show anonymous examples of good paragraphs and common errors.

UNIT REVIEW

Students can work in groups on this recap of the unit. For questions **2** and **3**, encourage students to check the relevant pages of the unit for the answers.

- Allow students time to answer the two questions in groups. For question **1**, ask students to explain why they chose that natural event. What do they want to find out?

BUILDING WONDERS

ACADEMIC TRACK
Architecture/Archaeology

ACADEMIC SKILLS
READING   Identifying relevant information
WRITING   Writing a comparison paragraph
GRAMMAR   Using comparative adjectives
CRITICAL THINKING   Interpreting quotes

UNIT OVERVIEW
The theme of this unit is architecture and how it relates to our culture and the values of civilizations.

- **READING 1:** The reading passage is about Gaudí's famous cathedral, La Sagrada Família; his inspirations from nature; and the long time frame for this project.
- **VIDEO:** The video describes the work of Brunelleschi, a clockmaker and goldsmith, who built the world's largest brick dome in Florence, Italy.
- **READING 2:** The reading passage describes two amazing structures from ancient times: Göbekli Tepe, a stone circle in Turkey, and Chichén Itzá, a Mayan city in Mexico.

Students draw on what they've read and watched to write a paragraph comparing two buildings. The unit prepares them by introducing vocabulary to talk about architecture and teaching them how to use comparison adjectives. They learn how to write a comparison paragraph and evaluate evidence. Lastly, students use a Venn diagram to help them plan their paragraphs, and then revise and edit their drafts—skills that students will use in every unit's *Writing Task*.

 THINK AND DISCUSS *(page 141)*
The questions help prepare students for the subject matter covered in the unit—architecture. The scene depicts the Taj Mahal, a magnificent building in India, in the early morning.
- Have students study the picture, title, and captions.
- Discuss the photo as a class. What do students think the photo and the unit are about? Provide your own overview.
- Discuss the two questions as a class. For question **1**, do students agree on the oldest/tallest buildings in your

area? If a computer is available, do an online search with the class. Are they surprised by the results? For question **2**, ask whether students have been to any of these buildings. If so, have them describe the experience.

ANSWER KEY

THINK AND DISCUSS
1. Answers will vary. Possible answers: The Empire State Building, Notre Dame, the Alhambra, the Parthenon, the Great Wall of China. They are special because of their place in history and their grandeur.
2. Answers will vary.

 EXPLORE THE THEME *(pages 142–143)*
The opening spread features information about the UNESCO world heritage sites and why these are important. It discusses the purposes of some monuments and mentions that for certain monuments, such as Stonehenge, we still don't know their purposes.
- Allow students time to study the spread and answer question **1** individually. Discuss reasons, and write a list on the board. Then have students read the information in the text.
- Have students discuss question **2** in pairs.
- Discuss answers as a class. Ask students to share why they chose these places.
- Have students answer the question in part **B**. Remind students to use the correct forms of the words.
- Elicit example sentences from students for each of the blue words.

ANSWER KEY

EXPLORE THE THEME
A 1. Answers will vary. Possible answers: to commemorate a person or an event, to symbolize power and wealth, to attract visitors, to display technical progress
  2. Answers will vary. Possible answer: I'd love to see Mount Rushmore because I really admire the presidents who are featured there.
B   religious; symbol; structure

Reading 1

PREPARING TO READ (page 144)

A Building Vocabulary

Students find the seven blue words in the passage and use contextual clues to guess the meanings. Remind students to look for the parts of speech to help them better understand the new words.

- Allow time for students to complete the exercise individually.
- Check answers as a class. What clues from the reading passage did students find helpful?
- Elicit example sentences for each vocabulary item. Ask: What is the theme of this chapter? Are you committed to your language learning? What inspired you to learn English? What is one famous sculpture? What do the pictures on page 128 illustrate?

See Vocabulary Extension 8A on page 210 of the Student Book for additional practice with Word Partners: adjective + style.

B Using Vocabulary

Students should practice using the new vocabulary items while answering the two questions.

- Have students discuss their answers in pairs.
- Compare answers as a class. Elicit example answers from students. For question **1**, ask students if they know of any famous architects from their country or countries. For question **2**, ask whether they like the building. Why or why not?

C Brainstorming

Students complete the chart with their ideas. Each idea should be brief. Read the example before students begin.

- Have students work in pairs to complete the exercise.
- Have them compare answers in groups of three or four.
- Draw the word web on the board, and elicit answers from different groups in the class. Ask students if they have seen any examples of the ideas from the word web on real buildings. If so, where?

ANSWER KEY

PREPARING TO READ

A 1. Sculpture
   2. committed to
   3. inspiration (Note: The verb is *inspire*.)
   4. theme
   5. architect (Note: The person is an *architect*; the field is *architecture*.)
   6. illustrate (Note: *Illustrate* often refers to drawings, but it can also refer to speech or writing.)
   7. style

B Answers will vary. Possible answers:
   1. Frank Lloyd Wright; Falling Water
   2. It's a brick school building. It is modern.

C Answers will vary. Possible answers:
   The sky: rooms with glass ceilings
   Animals: animal sculpted into the columns
   Water: The windows have stained glass that looks like waterfalls.
   Plants: The walls are painted to look like a jungle.

 Have students read the passage individually, or play the audio and have students read along.

OVERVIEW OF THE READING

The reading passage is about the famous Spanish architect Antoni Gaudí and his most famous building, La Sagrada Família Cathedral in Barcelona, which was unfinished at the time of his death in 1926. Construction work on this architectural wonder continues to this day.

Online search terms: virtual visit La Sagrada Família; Gaudí globotreks; works of Antoni Gaudí

UNDERSTANDING THE READING (page 149)

A Understanding Main Ideas

Students are asked to identify the purpose for each paragraph in the reading passage. Explain that *La Sagrada Família* refers to the Holy Family. *Timeless* means that something is so good or beautiful that it cannot be affected by changes in society or fashion. Elicit the meaning of *natural wonders*.

- Have students complete the activity individually.
- Have them check their answers in pairs.

- Check answers as a class. Ask students how they arrived at their answers.

B Understanding Details

Remind students that a chart is a useful way of seeing a lot of information at one time. Students test their understanding of the details in the passage by filling in the chart about the influences of nature on La Sagrada Família. Read the first example, and point out that students' answers can be brief. If necessary, direct them to paragraph D and the illustrations on page 147.

- Allow students time to complete the chart individually.
- Have them form pairs and compare their answers.
- Compare answers as a class. Ask which of these elements students would most like to see.

C Critical Thinking: Interpreting Quotes

The *Critical Thinking* box explains that quotes add credibility to a claim. First, elicit why it is important to have a credible source. Then explain that readers should also ask why the quote is important. Have students read the quotes and discuss their meaning. How are these related to the main idea of the passage? Students may need the first item done as an example.

- Have students discuss the quotes in pairs.
- Discuss the quotes as a class. Ask students whether they agree with the quotes. Why or why not? Is there one that they like more than the others? Why?

D Critical Thinking: Reflecting

Have students think about what they have read and discuss their personal opinions. Remind them to justify their opinions.

- Have students answer the questions individually.
- Have students discuss their answers in pairs.
- Discuss answers as a class. If any students have been to La Sagrada Família, ask them to describe the experience. If not, ask them to imagine what the experience would be like. What adjectives would they use to describe the structure?

Ideas for… EXPANSION

Have students research the work of modern architects from around the world. Have students work individually or in small groups to choose one architect and one building to present to the class. They should show photographs, give a brief biography of the architect, and explain what inspired the architect's work. Then they should explain why they like the building that they chose to present. After the presentations, students vote on the building that they like the best.

DEVELOPING READING SKILLS *(page 150)*

20 MINS

Reading Skill: Identifying Relevant Information

The *Reading Skill* box describes how to identify relevant information. It explains the importance of scanning for specific information, such as people, places, dates, and numbers. Have volunteers read the text in the box aloud. Elicit when people usually scan for information in their own lives. Remind students that numbers and capitalized letters can signal where to find this information.

A Matching

Each of the following questions is related to a specific type of information. Have students match these in preparation for exercise B below, in which they scan a paragraph for the information.

- Allow time for students to complete the task individually.
- Check answers as a class.

B Scanning

Students scan the paragraph to find the answers to the questions in exercise A. Remind students to look for capitalized words and numbers. They should underline the answers in the paragraph.

- Have students find their answers individually. Give students 1 or 2 minutes to find these answers. Remind students not to read every word in the paragraph.
- Have them form pairs and compare their answers.
- Check answers as a class. Ask if some answers were easier to find than others. If so, why?

C Identifying Relevant Information

Students scan the reading passage to find the answers to the questions. Remind students to look for capitalized words and numbers.

- Have students find the answers individually. Give students 1 or 2 minutes to find the answers. Remind students not to read every word.
- Have them form pairs and compare their answers.
- Check answers as a class. Ask students if they scanned from the beginning of the passage, or if they turned to the paragraphs where they thought they would find the information. Elicit that, based on the questions, they only needed to look at the introduction and the last section of the reading.

ANSWER KEY

DEVELOPING READING SKILLS

A 1. c; **2.** b; **3.** d; **4.** a

B Underlined words: <u>2,300 miles (3,700 kilometers);</u> <u>around A.D. 800; Polynesian islands; 13 feet (4 meters) tall</u>

C 1. 1926 (Paragraph E)
  2. Mark Burry (Paragraph E)
  3. 2026 (Paragraph G)

Video

VIEWING: A DARING DESIGN *(pages 151-152)*
40 MINS

Overview of the Video

The video describes the construction of Brunelleschi's dome in Florence, Italy. Brunelleschi has been called the first engineer of the Renaissance. With no formal training, he built the largest dome in the world.

Online search terms: Medici; Brunelleschi; Florence virtual tour; National Geographic Il Duomo

BEFORE VIEWING

A Learning about the Topic

The paragraph prepares students for the video by giving them background information about Florence, Italy. Ask if anyone has been to Florence. If so, what are some adjectives they would use to describe it?

- Have students complete the task individually.
- Discuss answers as a class. Ask: What do you expect Ponte Vecchio to look like? If computers are available, search online for pictures of the bridge and downtown Florence.

B Vocabulary in Context

This exercise introduces students to some of the key words used in the video. Remind students to try to infer the meanings from the context.

- Have students complete the task individually.
- Check answers as a class. Elicit example sentences for each word. Ask: What are other things that can be built out of bricks or cement? What objects can be semicircles? Do any rooms in this building have irregular shapes? If so, which ones?

ANSWER KEY

BEFORE VIEWING

A 1. buy jewelry and souvenirs
  2. Answers will vary. Possible answer: because the history and works of art can be seen all around the city (e.g., the architecture, streets, and gardens), not only inside the museums

B 1. irregular (Note: *Curved* means rounded or bending.)
  2. brick
  3. semicircle
  4. cement

WHILE VIEWING

A ▶ Understanding Main Ideas

Have students read the items silently before you play the video. Then have the students watch and check the items that are true. Elicit the meanings of *constructed, base, dome,* and *central support system* by pointing out the images at the bottom of the page.

- Have them complete the task while the video is playing.
- Have students form pairs and compare answers.
- Check answers as a class. Elicit the correct answers for the false statements.

B ▶ Understanding Details

Have students fill in any labels that they recall from the first viewing before playing the video a second time.

- Have students complete the task while the video is playing.
- Have students form pairs and compare answers.
- Check answers as a class. Ask if there are any other words that students need to have explained, and elicit definitions from volunteers.

ANSWER KEY

WHILE VIEWING

A   1, 3, 4, 6

B **1.** inner

   2. outer

   3. wood

   4. lift

   5. vertical

   6. ropes

AFTER VIEWING

A Reacting to the Video

Students should discuss the question based on the information they have learned in the video.

- Have students discuss the question in pairs.
- Discuss as a class. Ask the class what the benefits and drawbacks would be, and create a T-chart on the board.

Ideas for… EXPANSION

In pairs, have students draw comic strips of a tour through Florence. Each pair of students should draw important sights on a piece of paper. Assure students that they don't need to worry about making these look perfect; they can label the different parts. They should role play tour guide and tourist, then use their ideas to add stick figures and dialogue bubbles to their comic strips. When their work is completed, display the students' comic strips in the classroom. Allow time for students to read their classmates' comic strips. Afterward, ask students what they remember and like about the different comic strips.

B Critical Thinking: Synthesizing

Students draw on information from Reading 1 and the video to compare the two structures.

- Allow students time to answer the questions individually. Encourage students to take notes before writing sentences.
- Have students form pairs and compare the sentences they have written.
- Discuss as a class. Elicit example sentences and write them on the board. Ask: Do you prefer one of the two structures? Why?

ANSWER KEY

AFTER VIEWING

A   Answers will vary. Possible answer: This might have helped him "think outside the box. "For example, his idea of an inner and outer shell probably came from his experience as a clockmaker. A formally trained architect may not have been as creative as he was in coming up with a solution.

B   Answers will vary. Possible answers:

Brunelleschi's dome is in Italy, and La Sagrada Família is in Spain.

La Sagrada Família is taking longer to build than Brunelleschi's dome.

Brunelleschi's dome is older than La Sagrada Família.

Both structures have a religious purpose (i.e., to honor God).

Reading 2

PREPARING TO READ *(page 153)*

A Building Vocabulary

In this exercise, students read the sentences about culture and architecture. Then they choose the correct definition for the eight vocabulary words.

- Have students complete the exercise individually.
- Check answers as a class. Elicit example sentences for each vocabulary item. Ask: What is a common topic for debate? What is another example of a holy building? What did your breakfast consist of? How long does it usually take to construct a new building in your area?

See Vocabulary Extension 8B on page 210 of the Student Book for additional practice with Word Link: trans- *(meaning "across")*

B Using Vocabulary

Students should use the new vocabulary items while discussing the three questions.

- Have students work in pairs to answer the questions.
- Discuss answers as a class. Elicit example answers from students. Ask: What methods of transportation are used today? What methods were used in ancient times? Have volunteers describe temples that they have visited. Ask students whether their answers to question 3 were influenced by what they learned in the video. Why or why not?

C Predicting

Students scan the reading passage, focusing on dates and names of places.

- Students should write their answers individually. Give students 1 minute to find this information.
- Have students check answers in pairs.
- Have students compare their answers as a class. Ask students what else they hope to learn about these two places.

ANSWER KEY

PREPARING TO READ

A **1.** b; **2.** a; **3.** a; **4.** b; **5.** a; **6.** b; **7.** b; **8.** a

B Answers will vary. Possible answers:

  1. container ships; trains; trucks

  2. I've been to Angkor Wat in Cambodia. It's one of the most stunning places I've visited.

  3. An architect needs to be organized, and have good communication and visualization skills.

C Answers will vary. Possible answers: thousands of years old; temples for people to worship in

 Have students read the passage individually, or play the audio and have students read along.

OVERVIEW OF THE READING

The reading passage describes two ancient structures. Göbekli Tepe is a stone circle in Turkey, one of the oldest man-made structures on Earth. Chichén Itzá is an ancient Mayan city in Mexico that has pyramids, temples, and other structures.

Online search terms: Göbekli Tepe, Klaus Schmidt archaeologist; Chichén Itzá; Maya facts

UNDERSTANDING THE READING *(page 156)*

A Understanding the Main Idea

Students read the passage and then choose the best title from three options.

- Allow time for students to complete the task individually.
- Check answers as a class. Ask students how they arrived at their answers.

B Understanding Details

Students read the statements and decide which ones are true. If some students finish early, have them correct the false statements. As an alternative activity, have half of the students read about Göbekli Tepe and the other half read about Chichén Itzá. Then have them work together to compare the two places and answer the questions.

- Allow time for students to complete the task individually.
- Have students check answers in pairs.
- Check answers as a class. Ask students to correct the false statements.

C Identifying Evidence

Students read the passage again to find the purpose(s) the writer gives for each structure and the evidence the writer provides. You may want to complete the first item as a class.

- Allow students time to answer the questions individually.
- Have students check answers in pairs.
- Check answers with the class. Have students share their answers. Explain that they will discuss their ideas further when they use this information in exercise D below.

D Critical Thinking: Evaluating an Argument

Students reflect on the evidence given in the reading passage to evaluate the arguments.

- Have students refer to their answers in exercise C to support their ideas. For question 1, explain that levels of certainty are words that show how confident someone is that something is correct. Words such as *maybe, perhaps, could,* and *might* show that the writer is less certain.
- Allow students time to answer the questions in groups of three. Before beginning, tell the class how long you will give them to discuss these questions. Assign a role to each member of the group. One person should be the note taker, another should be the time checker (to keep the group on task), and a third should be the spokesperson (who will present the group's ideas to the class).
- Discuss as a class. Ask each group's spokesperson to share their group's ideas.

E Critical Thinking: Reflecting

Have students read the question and reflect on their own opinions. Encourage students to use their personal experience or knowledge of other historical sites as they justify their opinions.

- Allow time for students to discuss their ideas in pairs.
- Discuss answers as a class. Draw the Pros/Cons chart on the board. As students share their answers, write them on the chart. Have students assess the chart and decide if they think the pros outweigh the cons.

ANSWER KEY

UNDERSTANDING THE READING

A   b

B   2, 3, 6

C   Answers will vary. Possible answers:

Chichén Itzá

Purpose(s): a religious site, a place to make sacrifices to a god; a place to view Venus and other planets

Evidence: Spanish records; bones, jewelry, and other objects that people wore when they were sacrificed have been found.

Göbekli Tepe

Purpose(s): a holy meeting place; a feasting site

Evidence: The T-shaped pillars could represent human beings in a religious ceremony; animal bones and large containers for liquid have been found; smaller pillars similar to Göbekli Tepe's have been found farther away.

D   Answers will vary. Possible answers:

1. The language when the writer talks about Chichén Itzá is very certain: "Chichén Itzá was both," "records show," and "experts know." With Göbekli Tepe, the writer is less certain: "archaeologists are still debating," "new evidence suggests," and "it's as though."

2. I find the argument for Chichén Itzá more convincing because of the language used by the writer. Since Göbekli Tepe is much older, there is less evidence showing what happened there.

E   Answers will vary. Possible answers:

Pros: By visiting and studying these ancient sites, we can learn more about our past.

Cons: Too many tourists can damage a site physically, or make a special place feel overcrowded.

Ideas for… EXPANSION

Have students work in two large groups. One group represents a tourist organization hoping to promote tourism in Chichén Itzá and Göbekli Tepe. The other group wants to preserve these sites and only allow archaeologists to enter the sites. Give students 5 to 7 minutes to prepare their arguments. Then have the students who work for the tourist organization stand in a circle facing outward. Have each of the students who want to preserve the sites stand facing one of the members of the other group. Explain that they will debate their case one on one. After 1 minute, the students in the outside circle move one step clockwise, so each student is speaking with another person. Repeat this, switching every 1 to 2 minutes, at least four times. Ask students if they felt their argument improved after the fourth debate. When the class has completed this exercise, have students vote on which group they agree with.

Writing

OVERVIEW

In this section, students prepare to write a comparison paragraph about two structures. The lesson starts by teaching students how to use comparison adjectives. Students then learn how to write a comparison paragraph. In the *Writing Task*, students apply these lessons by brainstorming, planning, and writing about two structures. As added support, they will encounter two drafts of sample paragraphs and revising strategies that the author used. Students will use a checklist to revise their own paragraphs. Editing practice helps students correct common mistakes with comparative adjectives. After this, students write the final drafts of their paragraphs.

EXPLORING WRITTEN ENGLISH (pages 157-159)

A Noticing

Students are expected to notice how comparative adjectives are used by reading the information and filling in the box with the correct comparative form. This exercise is to be done before going over the information in the *Language for Writing* box. Point out that they will only use three of the four options in the box.
- Have students complete the task individually.
- Check answers as a class. Ask volunteers to read the sentences aloud.

Language for Writing: Using Comparative Adjectives

The *Language for Writing* box describes how to use comparative adjectives. It explains why we use comparative adjectives and how to form them: adjective + -er + *than*; *more/less* + adjective + *than*; and *(not) as* + adjective + *as*. Have students read the *Language for Writing* box. Have students look again at exercise A and rewrite the sentences using a different comparative adjective structure. Elicit: Stonehenge is *newer than* Göbekli Tepe. Or Stonehenge is *not as old as* Göbekli Tepe. Allow time for students to write the sentences. Then write them on the board.

B Language for Writing

Students practice writing comparative adjective sentences. They should read the information provided and then complete the sentences to reflect the information.

- Allow students time to complete the activity individually.
- Have them check answers in pairs.
- Check answers as a class.

C Language for Writing

Students create their own sentences using comparative adjectives. Before beginning the exercise, you may want make two lists on the board: interesting places and descriptive adjectives. Be sure to keep these ideas brief.
- Allow students time to complete the task individually.
- Have students read the sentences they created in groups of three or four. Have each group check the grammar and then choose the three sentences to write on the board.
- Compare and correct the sentences on the board as a class.

Ideas for... EXPANSION

Have students work in pairs to write three true sentences and one false sentence comparing buildings in the area in which the class is being taught. Each sentence should include a different form of a comparative adjective from the *Language Writing* box. Have students read their sentences to the class. The class should decide which sentence is false.

See Grammar Summary on page 222 of the Student Book for additional practice with using comparative adjectives.

ANSWER KEY

EXPLORING WRITTEN ENGLISH

A 1. older than
   2. not as old as
   3. less expensive than

LANGUAGE FOR WRITING

B 1. taller than
   2. as tall as
   3. more traditional than
   4. not as long as
   5. higher than

C Answers will vary. Possible answers:
   1. Los Angeles isn't as compact as Boston.
   2. The climate in Riyadh is hotter than the climate in Reykjavik.
   3. Tokyo is more expensive to live in than Mexico City.

Writing Skill: Writing a Comparison Paragraph

The *Writing Skill* box describes the steps to take to write a comparison paragraph. The *Writing Skill* box teaches students to choose a topic, think of the points they want to discuss, and then think of details about each of those points. The box lists transition words for similarities and differences. Have students read the text in the *Writing Skill* box aloud. Ask students which of these words they already know. Elicit why students should try to use a variety of transition words in their writing. (It makes it more interesting; it improves the flow of the paragraph.)

D Writing Skill

Students read the paragraph and compare the ways that the two libraries are similar and different. They add this information to the Venn diagram. If necessary, remind them of the structure of a Venn diagram. Elicit one example for the Barrett Library and one example of something that the two libraries share.

- Allow students time to complete the task individually.
- Have students check answers in pairs.
- Draw the Venn diagram on the board, and ask volunteers to add answers to the circles.
- Check answers as a class.

E Writing Skill

Students read the paragraph again and answer the questions.

- Have students complete the task individually.
- Have students check their answers in pairs.
- Check answers as a class. For question 2, elicit why detail sentences are necessary. (They support the points of comparison.) For question 3, make a list of the comparison words that were used.

ANSWER KEY

WRITING SKILL

D   Answers will vary. Possible answers:

The Grant Library: built in 1890, classical style with marble columns like a Greek temple, open 24 hours a day

Intersecting area: used for student research, part of a college campus, both have books available for students to use, both are libraries

The Barrett Library: modern design, built in early 20th century, craftsman style, made of wood, library and museum, open 7 hours a day

---

E 1. style and purpose

   2. and **3.** The Grant Library and the Barrett Library are (both) important resources for student research at my university, but there are some differences between the two structures. First, the buildings have very different styles. <u>The Grant Library, built in 1890, is older than the Barrett Library and was built in the classical style</u>. For example, there are tall marble columns at the entrance, which make the library look like a Greek temple. The Barrett Library, (on the other hand) has a more modern design. <u>It was built in the early 20th century in the craftsman style and is made entirely of wood</u>. The purposes of the two libraries are also different. <u>The Barrett Library also functions as a museum, so it's open only seven hours a day</u>. <u>The Grant Library, (however) is open 24 hours a day, so students can do research or study there for a longer time</u>. The two buildings have different styles and purposes, but (both) are excellent examples of the variety of architectural styles at my university.

WRITING TASK *(page 160)*

A Planning

Remind students that planning is an important step for gathering ideas before writing. Read the *Goal* box aloud so students will be familiar with the writing task before planning. Provide one or two example ideas. Have students follow steps 1 to 4 to choose two buildings, plan their points of comparison, fill in the Venn diagram, and write a topic sentence. Have a student read the steps aloud. Remind students that complete sentences are not necessary in the Venn diagram.

- Allow time for students to complete their outlines individually. Provide assistance as needed.
- Have students share their ideas in pairs and offer feedback to each other.

B First Draft

Have students write first drafts of their paragraphs based on their outlines.

- Allow time for students to complete the task individually. Provide assistance as needed. Refrain from error correction at this point.

WRITING TASK

A   Answers will vary. Possible answers:

Golden Gate Bridge: 1.7 miles long; opened in 1937

Both: amazing engineering; similar design; steel suspension bridges; tall towers

Brooklyn Bridge: 5,989 feet long; opened in 1883

Point 1: design

Point 2: length

Point 3: date of completion

Topic Sentence: The Golden Gate Bridge and the Brooklyn Bridge are both examples of amazing engineering.

REVISING PRACTICE *(page 161)*

The *Revising Practice* box contains an exercise that demonstrates several ways students can improve their first drafts.

- Allow time for students to analyze the two drafts and complete the exercise.
- Check answers as a class. Ask students to identify each change and explain how it makes the revised draft stronger.

C Revised Draft

Students should apply the revision techniques used in the *Revising Practice* box to their own drafts, where applicable.

- Explain to students that they will be using the questions as a guide for checking and improving their drafts.
- As a class, go over the questions carefully to make sure students understand them.
- Allow students time to revise their paragraphs.

EDITING PRACTICE *(page 162)*

The *Editing Practice* box trains students to spot and correct common errors related to comparative adjectives. As a class, go over the information in the box carefully.

- Allow students time to complete the exercise individually.
- Check answers in pairs.
- Check answers as a class by asking students to read their corrected sentences aloud and explain the errors.

REVISING PRACTICE

a, d, b, a, c

EDITING PRACTICE

1. The Seville Cathedral <u>is smaller than</u> St. Peter's Basilica.
2. In my opinion, La Sagrada Família is <u>more attractive than</u> St. Mary's Cathedral.
3. The Temple of Angkor Wat in Cambodia is <u>not as ancient as</u> the Borobudur Temple in Indonesia.
4. Göbekli Tepe is <u>older than</u> the Parthenon in Greece.
5. The Tokyo Skytree is <u>not as tall as</u> the Burj Khalifa in Dubai, which has a height of almost 2,723 feet (830 meters).
6. The construction of the Barrett Library was <u>less expensive than</u> the construction of the Morrison Library.
7. The Brooklyn Bridge is not as <u>long as</u> the Golden Gate Bridge.

D Final Draft

Have students apply the skills taught in *Editing Practice* to their own revised drafts and check for any other errors.

- Allow time for students to work individually on editing their drafts.
- Walk around and monitor students as they work. Provide assistance as needed.
- Collect their work once they have completed it.
- For the next class, show anonymous examples of good paragraphs and common errors.

UNIT REVIEW
10 MINS

Students can work in groups on this recap of the unit. For question 1, encourage students to use the target words when appropriate. For questions **2** and **3**, encourage them to check the relevant pages of the unit for answers.

- Allow students time to answer the three questions in groups. For question **1**, ask groups if they changed their opinions as they studied this unit.
- As a class, have students vote for the structure or building they would most like to visit.

FORM AND FUNCTION

9

ACADEMIC TRACK

Life Science

ACADEMIC SKILLS

READING	Identifying theories
WRITING	Writing a summary paragraph
GRAMMAR	Using synonyms
CRITICAL THINKING	Evaluating evidence

UNIT OVERVIEW

The theme of this unit is nature. The title, "Form and Function," refers to the animals' adaptations over time and the use of biomimetics, drawing on nature to inspire new inventions.

- **READING 1:** This reading discusses the evolution of feathers, from the time of the dinosaur "theropod" to the present day.

- **VIDEO:** The video presents descriptions of the flying tree snake and the Draco lizard. These are animals that fly, or rather glide, through the forest to escape predators.

- **READING 2:** This reading gives examples of biomimetics—how shark scales and toucan bills have inspired modern designs of cars, airplanes, and bathing suits, among other things.

Students draw on what they've read and watched to write a summary paragraph about a section of the reading passage. The unit prepares them by introducing vocabulary to talk about nature and evaluating evidence. It explains the importance of using synonyms and the organization of a summary paragraph. Lastly, it reviews brainstorming and planning techniques.

 THINK AND DISCUSS *(page 163)*

The scene depicts a male bird of paradise spreading his feathers. It is meant to show that this unit will be about nature, and more specifically, animals and their unique characteristics.

- Have students study the picture, title, and captions.
- Discuss the photo as a class. What do students think the photo and the unit are about? Provide your own overview.

- Discuss the two questions as a class. For question **1**, elicit examples of animals, and then discuss the reasons. For question **2**, allow students time to think of as many man-made objects as possible. Offer an example (Gaudí's La Sagrada Família in Unit 8), and create a list on the board.

ANSWER KEY

THINK AND DISCUSS

Answers will vary. Possible answers:

1. Polar bears have fur to keep them warm. Elephants have wrinkly skin that helps them stay cool. Snakes have scales that protect their bodies and help them to move along the ground.

2. Velcro (inspired by a plant), sonar (inspired by the use of echolocation by bats and dolphins), airplane design (based on wings of birds)

 EXPLORE THE THEME *(pages 164–165)*

The opening spread provides information about animal and plant adaptation.

- Allow time for students to read the spread and answer the questions individually.
- Check answers as a class. Ask students for examples of how other animals have adapted to their environments.
- Elicit example sentences from students for each of the blue words.

ANSWER KEY

EXPLORE THE THEME

A 1. **Physical adaptation:** desert plants that store water in their stems. **Behavioral adaptation:** gray whales that give birth in warm water but travel to cold water for food.

Answers will vary. Possible answers:

2. **Behavioral adaptation:** nocturnal animals, such as bats, can avoid competition from birds and hide from predators. **Physical adaptation:** the panda uses a "false thumb" to eat bamboo.

B evolve; theory; characteristic

Reading 1

PREPARING TO READ (page 166)

A Building Vocabulary

The sentences are definitions for the words in the reading passage on pages 167–168. They contain seven key vocabulary items that appear in the passage. Students should use contextual clues to deduce the meanings of the words. Remind students to use the correct word forms.

- Have students work individually to complete the exercise.
- Have students check answers in pairs.
- Check answers as a class. Ask: What do detectives look for when they are working on a case? (Elicit *clues* and *evidence*.) What's something that is on display in a nearby store window? Do you wear more layers of clothing in the winter or the summer?

See Vocabulary Extension 9A on page 211 of the Student Book for additional practice with Word Partners: adjective + advantage.

B Using Vocabulary

Students should use the new vocabulary items while discussing the two questions.

- Have students work in pairs to discuss the questions.
- Discuss answers as a class. Elicit example answers from students. Make a list of strategies that animals use on the board. Ask: Are any of these strategies also used by humans?

C Brainstorming

Students should write the main characteristics of birds. Each idea should be brief. If available, show images of different types of birds in nature. Have a student read the example aloud.

- Have students work individually.
- Have them form pairs and compare answers.
- Elicit answers from the class, and make a word web on the board with the answers.

D Predicting

The opening paragraph discusses the fact that feathers have existed for millions of years. Remind students to skim the first paragraph but also look at the title, captions, and subheads to predict what the article is about. Elicit the meanings of *paleontologist* and *fossil* by directing students to the first footnote on page 167. Elicit the meaning of *insulation* (materials used to keep something warm). Explain that they do not need to give answers based on the passage; they should use their own ideas.

- Give students 1 minute to skim the first paragraph and look at the title, captions, and subheads.
- Have students discuss ideas in pairs.
- Discuss as a class. Write students' ideas on the board. Revisit these categories after completing the reading.

ANSWER KEY

PREPARING TO READ

A 1. Evidence
2. layer
3. flexible
4. advantage
5. clue
6. display
7. attracts

B Answers will vary. Possible answers:
1. Darwin's theory of evolution, Einstein's theory of relativity
2. make special sounds or noises; show off their feathers; fight other animals to show their strength

C Answers will vary. Possible answers:
2. Birds build nests.
3. Birds have feathers.
4. Birds have beaks.

D Answers will vary. Possible answers:
Insulation: Feathers trap body heat to help birds stay warm.
Attraction: Colorful feathers help birds attract the opposite sex.
Flight: The shape and arrangement of feathers in wings help birds fly.

🎧 2.07 Have students read the passage individually, or play the audio and have students read along.

OVERVIEW OF THE READING

The passage is about the evolution of feathers, from dinosaurs to present-day birds, and theories about the different functions that feathers have.

Online search terms: birds of paradise project; theropod BBC; flamingo National Geographic

UNDERSTANDING THE READING *(page 169)*

A Understanding the Main Idea

Students are asked to choose the main idea of the reading passage.

- Have students complete the activity individually.
- Check answers as a class. Ask students how they arrived at their answers.

B Identifying Details

Students test their understanding of the details in the passage by completing the chart. Remind students of their answers to exercise D on page 166. Explain that this chart asks them to find fossil evidence as well. Elicit the meanings of: *the opposite sex* (for males, females; for females, males), *at an angle* (not straight), *movable* (can be moved), and *fold its arms* (cross arms close to its body).

- Allow students time to write their answers individually.
- Have them check their answers in pairs.
- Discuss answers as a class. Draw the chart on the board, and write students' answers.

C Critical Thinking: Evaluating Evidence

The *Critical Thinking* box explains the importance of evaluating evidence. Ask students if they remember what they learned from the *Critical Thinking* boxes on page 127 and page 149. Then have a student read the text in the box aloud. Write "Relevant, Logical, and Sufficient" on the board. Remind students to ask whether each theory meets these criteria.

- Allow time for students to discuss the questions in pairs.
- Discuss answers as a class. For each theory, have students decide whether it is relevant, logical, and sufficient. Ask students if their ideas about question **3** have changed after the discussion. Why or why not?

ANSWER KEY

UNDERSTANDING THE READING

A b

B Answers will vary. Possible answers:

INSULATION

Modern Examples: <u>young; soft feathers</u>

Fossil Evidence: Theropod fossils show that they used their front limbs to cover their nests, possibly to keep their young warm.

ATTRACTION

Modern Examples: Peacocks spread their brightly colored tails to attract peahens.

Fossil Evidence: Very small sacs inside theropod feathers, called melanosomes, give feathers their color and look the same as those in the feathers of birds today.

FLIGHT

Modern Examples: <u>thin and hard; long and flexible; bone</u>

Fossil Evidence: <u>movable bone</u>

C Answers will vary. Possible answers:

1. Yes, I think the fossil evidence helps. For example, there is a clear link between theropod melanosomes and the colored feathers of modern birds (attraction theory).

2. I think the writer could have provided more fossil evidence for the insulation theory.

3. I find the theory about insulation the least convincing. Theropods could have covered their nests with their front limbs for another reason (e.g., to protect their young from predators). The theory about flight is the most convincing to me because of the bone structure evidence. Also, it is logical that birds' ability to fly evolved over time.

DEVELOPING READING SKILLS *(page 170)*

Reading Skill: Identifying Theories

The *Reading Skill* box explains how to identify theories. Ask students why it is important to identify signals that indicate that a writer is talking about a theory. Elicit that it alerts the reader that the information has not been verified as fact; the writer is presenting possible theories. Have a student read the text in the box aloud. Then make a list of more words on the board. Add a column for verbs that show certainty as well (*know/proved/found*).

A Identifying Theories

Ask students to look at the picture and describe what they see. Elicit the meaning of limbs (arms and legs). Ask what they know about dinosaurs, and elicit that because the animals lived so long ago, it is hard to be certain about their lives. Then have students find the theories and circle the words that introduce them. You may want to do the first as an example.

- Allow time for students to complete the task individually.
- Have students form pairs and compare their answers.

- Check answers as a class. If possible, project the information on the board, and circle or underline as a class. Ask students to evaluate the theories based on the criteria in the *Critical Thinking* box on page 169. Do they think there is enough evidence to support these ideas?

B Identifying Theories

Students locate two theories in the reading passage and circle the words that introduce them. Encourage students to review the explanation in the *Reading Skills* box for clarification.

- Allow students time to complete the task individually.
- Have them form pairs and compare their answers.
- Write answers on the board.

Ideas for… EXPANSION

If it is available, show the trailer of the movie *Jurassic Park*. Ask students whether they have seen this movie. If so, ask students to describe what it is about. If not, ask what they notice about the trailer. What do they think it will be about? What will be fact and what will be theory? Why? Have students discuss these questions in groups of three or four and then share their answers with the class.

ANSWER KEY

DEVELOPING READING SKILLS

A Many scientists (think) that <u>a group of dinosaurs closely related to today's birds took the first steps toward flight when their limbs evolved to flap as they ran.</u> They (theorize) that <u>this arm flapping eventually led to flying.</u> . . . Instead, they (believe) <u>this animal flew by gliding from tree to tree.</u> They (speculate) that <u>the feathers formed a sort of parachute that helped the animal stay in the air.</u>

… Some researchers (suggest) that <u>M. gui's feathers weren't</u> <u>useful for flight at all.</u> They (think) that <u>the feathers possibly helped the animal to attract a mate, or made the tiny dinosaur look bigger.</u>

B Answers will vary. Possible answers:

1. They (think) this shows that <u>the dinosaurs were using feathers to keep their young warm.</u>

2. According to scientists, this common characteristic (suggests) that <u>feathered dinosaurs such as Anchiornis evolved flight by moving their feathered arms up and down as they ran, or by jumping from tree to tree.</u>

Video

VIEWING: FLYING REPTILES
(pages 171-172)

Overview of the Video

The video describes two animals that glide: the flying tree snake and the Draco lizard. It explains how they are able to glide through the air, and why they have evolved to do so.

Online search terms: flying fish; flying squirrel; Draco lizard; flying tree snake

BEFORE VIEWING

A Predicting

Students think of theories for how the reptiles glide. Elicit the meaning of *glide* and *reptile*, using the pictures as reference.

- Have students study the photo, title, and captions.
- Have students discuss their ideas with a partner.
- Discuss as a class. Ask students whether any of them has seen any of these animals before. If so, what adjectives would they use to describe them? If not, would they like to see them? Why or why not?

B Learning About the Topic

The paragraph prepares students for the video by giving them background information about some animals that can glide through the air. Different animals are featured in the video. Explain that they will have to infer the answer to question **2**.

- Have students complete the task individually.
- Have students check their answers in pairs.
- Check answers to question **1** as a class. Explain the meaning of *paws*. Discuss question **2**. If a computer is available, search online for videos of flying squirrels and flying fish.

C Vocabulary in Context

This exercise introduces students to some of the key words used in the video.

- Have students complete the task individually.
- Check answers as a class. Elicit example sentences for each word. Ask: What is a cat's usual prey? What is a place that people want to escape from? What is something that can be launched into the air?

BEFORE VIEWING

A Answers will vary. Possible answers:

The Draco lizard looks like it's wearing a cape, which helps it glide through the trees.

The snake looks like it's swinging and ready to launch itself from the tree.

B 1. Flying squirrels use their tails and a layer of skin connecting their paws; flying fish use their fins.

2. Answers will vary. Possible answers: wind speed; how high in the trees they are (for flying squirrels); size of fins (for flying fish)

C 1. escape

2. launch

3. prey

WHILE VIEWING

A ▶ Understanding the Main Idea

Have students read the question before you play the video. Tell students to write their answers in their own words. Ask whether any students have ever gone hang-gliding. If so, what did it feel like? If not, would they like to go?

• Have them complete the task while the video is playing.

• Compare answers as a class. Write two student definitions on the board, and ask students to work together to write a clear definition.

B ▶ Understanding Details

Have students read the statements and recall which are true or false from the first viewing before playing the video a second time.

• Have students complete the task while the video is playing.

• Check answers as a class. Have students correct the false answers.

Ideas for... EXPANSION

Have students choose an interesting animal that has adapted to its surroundings and find out more about it. Have students obtain basic information: where the animal lives, what it eats, what it looks like, and other interesting facts. Then have students describe how the animal has adapted to escape from predators, to catch its prey, or to survive in a particular environment. Have students write a paragraph about the animal and share what they have learned with the class.

WHILE VIEWING

A Answers will vary. Possible answer: The two animals can glide. Gliding is like flying but without going up in the air. It means starting out high, and moving through the air until landing at a lower spot.

B 1. T

2. T

3. T

4. F (Note: The Draco lizard is prey for the paradise tree snake.)

5. F (Note: 10 meters)

AFTER VIEWING

A Reacting to the Video

Students are asked to reflect on the information in the video and relate this to the more general statement.

• Allow students time to discuss the questions in pairs.

• Discuss as a class. Ask students to evaluate their classmates' theories. Are they relevant, logical, and sufficient? Which theory is the most convincing?

B Critical Thinking: Inferring Meaning

Students read the quote and decide on its meaning. Encourage students to recall the scene from the video. If necessary, play the scene again.

• Have students write their answers.

• Discuss as a class. Elicit example answers from students and write them on the board.

AFTER VIEWING

A Answers will vary. Possible answer: because gliding is the most efficient way to move from tree to tree in the rain forest.

B Answers will vary. Possible answer: The snake isn't frightened by the lizard's warning. It still wants to eat the lizard.

Reading 2

PREPARING TO READ (page 173)

A Building Vocabulary

The eight words in the box are related to the reading passage on pages 174–175. Students should use contextual clues to deduce the meanings of the words and complete the sentences with the correct words. Remind students to use the correct forms of the words.

- Have students complete the task individually.
- Check answers as a class. Elicit example sentences for each vocabulary item. Ask: How do you adjust to a new culture? Are you involved in any school activities? Do you prefer chocolate that is solid or hollow?

See Vocabulary Extension 9B on page 211 of the Student Book for additional practice with Word Link: pro- (meaning "in front/before").

B Using Vocabulary

Students should use the new vocabulary items while discussing the two questions. Point out that question **1** is difficult, and behavioral scientists have been discussing this for years. Students might want to use levels of certainty when discussing their answers. Elicit the meanings of *rough* and *smooth*.

- Have students work in pairs to answer the questions.
- Discuss answers as a class. Elicit example answers from students.

C Predicting

Students should look at the photos and read the subheads to make their own guesses about this reading. Stress that students should not try to read the entire passage; they should think of their own ideas You may want to give them 1 minute to skim the material.

- Have students look at the photos and subheads and answer the questions.
- Have students form pairs and compare their answers.
- Discuss answers as a class. Write a list on the board, and revisit it after reading the passage.

ANSWER KEY

PREPARING TO READ

A 1. process
   2. industry
   3. involved
   4. vary
   5. adjust
   6. solid
   7. surface
   8. unique

B   Answers will vary. Possible answers:

   1. We wear clothing; we can imagine things; we can voice our opinion and create change in the world.
   2. The walls have rough surfaces. The desks have smooth surfaces.

C   Answers will vary. Possible answers:

   Toucan bills and car safety: Maybe toucan bills are very hard, so cars can be made of a similar hard material.

   Shark scales and swimsuits: Shark scales must work well in the water, so they could be used as a model for swimsuit design.

 **2.08** Have students read the passage individually, or play the audio and have students read along.

OVERVIEW OF THE READING

The reading passage describes different examples of biomimetics. The passage discusses the functions of the toucan bill and shark skin in nature and how these functions can be reproduced to design better objects for humans.

Online search terms: National Geographic biomimetics; toucan bills biomimicry

UNDERSTANDING THE READING (page 176)

A Understanding the Main Idea

Students write a definition of the term biomimetics.

- Have students write a definition in pairs.
- Check answers as a class. Have two volunteers write their definitions on the board. Work as a class to create a class definition for the term.

B Identifying Details

Students are asked to find the purpose of the animal part and the products that are designed based on this animal part. Ask students if they were correct in their earlier predictions about the items.

- Allow time for students to complete the task individually.
- Have students check their answers in pairs.
- Check answers as a class. Draw the chart on the board and fill it in as a class.

C Identifying Theories

Students should reread paragraph B and identify three theories. They should underline the theories and circle the words used to introduce them. Offer the first as an example, if necessary.

- Allow students time to find the theories individually.
- Have them form pairs and compare their answers.
- Discuss as a class. Have volunteers read the theories aloud. Write the words that introduce the theories on the board.

D Critical Thinking: Applying

Students should identify what makes an invention an example of biomimetics. If necessary, have them review their definition from exercise A again.

- Allow students time to answer the questions individually.
- Have students discuss their answers in pairs. Have them justify the reasons for their choices.
- Discuss as a class. Does everyone agree? Why or why not?

E Critical Thinking: Synthesizing

Students should identify three animals and discuss how they are uniquely adapted to their environments. Encourage students to review the reading and their notes on the video again.

- Allow students time to answer the questions individually.
- Have them discuss their answers in pairs.
- Discuss as a class. Make word web with the animals and the ways that they are uniquely adapted to their environments.

Ideas for… EXPANSION

If computers are available, have students look online for examples of biomimicry. They should research one example and describe what they know about the animal, what the purpose of the animal part is in nature, and how the animal part will be used in a product. Students should present the information to the class and show images, if available. Then have the class vote on the example of biomimicry that they think could be the most useful.

ANSWER KEY

UNDERSTANDING THE READING

A Answers will vary. Possible answer: a process in which characteristics of animals are used to design new products for humans

B **TOUCAN BILLS**

Purposes: to attract mates, cut open fruit, fight, warn predators to stay away, control body temperature

Products/Technologies: panels in cars and planes to make them safer

SHARK SCALES

Purposes: to protect the shark, keep it clean, and help it swim quickly

Products/Technologies: coating for airplanes and ship bottoms, and swimwear that reduces drag

C Charles Darwin (theorized) that these bills attract mates. Other researchers (think) that the large bills are used for cutting fruit, for fighting, or for warning predators to stay away. A new study (suggests) that the enormous bills help control body temperature…

D 2, 3 (Explanation: Sentences 2 and 3 are examples of biomimetics because they make something new by copying nature. Sentences 1 and 4 are ways of using animal parts, not copying their form or structure.)

E Answers will vary. Possible answers:

The desert beetle has adapted to living in the desert by collecting water in its shell.

The Draco lizard has developed thin folds of skin that extend from its body to help it glide between trees.

The flying fish has developed long fins to help it glide over water.

Writing

OVERVIEW

In this section, students write a summary paragraph. The lesson starts by reviewing use of synonyms and then teaches students about writing a summary paragraph. In the *Writing Task*, students apply these lessons by writing a summary paragraph about one of the sections of the reading passage on pages 174–175. As added support, they will encounter two drafts of a sample paragraph. Students begin the task by brainstorming and planning their summary paragraphs. Students then draft their paragraphs, improve their drafts, and correct common mistakes that occur with synonyms.

EXPLORING WRITTEN ENGLISH *(pages 177-179)*

A Noticing

While completing the exercise, students are expected to notice that the simple past tense can be used for events that began and ended in the past. This exercise is to be done before going over the information in the *Language for Writing* box. Point out that the sentences are all excerpts from Readings **1** and **2**.
- Have students complete the task individually.
- Check answers as a class. Have students review the sentences in the reading passages to find the answers.

Language for Writing: Using Synonyms

The *Language for Writing* box gives examples of using synonyms to paraphrase a passage. Elicit what synonyms are by asking for other words that mean *big*, *small*, etc. Have students read the text in the box aloud. Point out the importance of choosing the right synonym from a possible list. Elicit that often the best synonyms are words that students already know. If possible, bring in a thesaurus or find one online. Have students check for possible alternatives to common words.

B Language for Writing

Students read the sentences and choose the best synonym for each. Explain that both of the word choices are synonyms, but only one is appropriate in this context. If a dictionary is available, allow students to use it.
- Allow students time to complete the activity individually.
- Have them check answers in pairs.
- Check answers as a class.

C Language for Writing

Students write four sentences from the reading passages and paraphrase them.
- Allow students time to complete the task individually.
- Have students compare their answers with a partner.
- Ask volunteers to share their answers with the class. Write two to three examples on the board. Ask volunteers whether they used synonyms.

Writing Skill: Writing a Summary Paragraph

The *Writing Skill* box explains the key characteristics of a summary. The *Writing Skill* box teaches students to find the key ideas, and then write them in their own words. Emphasize that the list of characteristics is important for this type of writing. Have a student read these aloud.

D Writing Skill

Students should read the paragraph and highlight the key ideas. Remind students that they will be doing this in order to write a summary paragraph.
- Allow students time to complete the task individually.
- Have students form pairs and compare answers.
- Compare answers as a class. Ask students why they chose to underline certain ideas and not others.

E Writing Skill

Students read the key ideas from the paragraph in exercise D and number these in the correct order. Point out that the sentences have the same ideas as those in the paragraph but have been rewritten.

- Allow time for students to complete the task individually.
- Have students form pairs and compare answers.
- Check answers as a class.

F Writing Skill

Have students rewrite the sentences in exercise E in paragraph form. Have students find synonyms for the underlined words. Encourage students to use a thesaurus, and point out that often a simple word fits well.

- Allow time for students to complete the task individually.
- Have students form pairs and compare answers.
- Have a volunteer read the paragraph aloud to the class. On the board, write a list of synonyms for each underlined word.

Ideas for… EXPANSION

Have students choose a reading passage from a previous unit in this book. Have them skim the passage again to remind themselves of the details, and then close the book and free-write about the passage. Remind students to include the main idea of the passage and some key details. Once they have written a paragraph, have them return to the reading passage and see if there are more details they would like to add. Point out that it is often easier to summarize without having the article available at the same time. Emphasize that this summary paragraph should follow the criteria listed in the *Writing Skill* box. Have volunteers read their paragraphs aloud.

ANSWER KEY

WRITING SKILL

D Answers will vary. Possible answers:

<u>Scientists are studying the adaptations of living organisms in order to use their designs in products and technologies for humans.</u> This field of study is known as <u>biomimetics</u>. <u>Velcro is one example of biomimetics.</u> <u>In 1948, a Swiss engineer named George de Mestral removed a bur stuck to his dog's fur.</u> De Mestral studied it under a microscope and noticed how well the hooks on the bur stuck to things. <u>He copied the design to make a two-piece fastening device.</u> . . .

E 3, 2, 4, 1

F Answers will vary. Possible answers:

Biomimetics involves studying the ways in which <u>plants and animals</u> adapt to their environments in order to develop useful products and technologies for <u>people</u>. An example of biomimetics is Velcro. A Swiss engineer, George de Mestral, <u>saw</u> how well a bur <u>clung</u> to his dog's fur. He <u>created</u> a two-part fastener by mimicking the hooks on the bur and the softness of his dog's fur.

WRITING TASK (page 180)
40 MINS

A Brainstorming

Remind students that brainstorming is a useful first step for gathering ideas before writing. Read the *Goal* box aloud so students will be familiar with the writing task before brainstorming. Have them list as many details as they can remember about the two topics. Ideas should be briefly worded. They need not be listed in any order.

- Have students complete the task individually. Set a time limit so that students are motivated to write quickly.
- Compare answers in pairs.
- Compare answers as a class.

B Planning

Students choose a section of one of the reading passages to summarize and write the title. They should reread that section and then write a topic sentence and key ideas. Remind students that complete sentences are not necessary. Refer them to the *Writing Skill* box on page 178 for more details about writing a summary paragraph.

- Allow time for students to complete their outlines individually. Provide assistance as needed.

C First Draft

Have students write first drafts of their paragraphs based on their outlines.

- Allow time for students to complete the task individually. Provide assistance as needed. Refrain from error correction at this point.

WRITING TASK

A   Answers will vary. Possible answers:

Toucan Bills and Car Safety: made of keratin, strong and light, absorbs impact so would be good for cars.

Shark Scales and Swimsuits: look like little teeth; very flexible; make sharks go faster because of less drag, so they can make swimmers in bathing suits go faster too.

B   Answers will vary. Model answers:

Title of Original Text: Animal Adaptation

Topic Sentence: An adaptation is a change in a plant or an animal.

Key Ideas:

Changes are a result of mutation.

More organisms inherit a mutation; eventually becomes a normal characteristic of the species.

Two kinds of adaptation: physical and behavioral.

Desert plant that can store its own water = physical adaptation.

Whale migration = behavioral adaptation.

REVISING PRACTICE   *(page 181)*

The *Revising Practice* box contains an exercise that demonstrates several ways students can improve their first drafts.

- Allow time for students to analyze the two drafts and complete the exercise. Point out that one of the types of changes (*a-d*) can be used more than once.
- Check answers as a class. Ask students to identify each change and explain how it makes the revised draft stronger.

D Revised Draft

Students should apply the revision techniques used in the *Revising Practice* box to their own drafts, where applicable.

- Explain to students that they will be using the questions as a guide for checking and improving their drafts.
- As a class, go over the questions carefully to make sure students understand them.
- Allow students time to revise their paragraphs.

EDITING PRACTICE   *(page 182)*

The *Editing Practice* box trains students to spot and correct common errors related to synonyms. As a class, go over the information in the box carefully to make sure students understand what to look out for.

- Allow students time to complete the exercise individually.
- Check answers as a class by asking students to read their corrected sentences aloud and explain the errors.

REVISING PRACTICE

b, a, a, d, c

EDITING PRACTICE

1. elegant
2. light
3. young
4. spread
5. shell
6. helpful
7. leaves

E Final Draft

Have students apply the skills taught in *Editing Practice* to their own revised drafts, and check for any other errors.

- Allow time for students to work individually on editing their drafts.
- Walk around and monitor students as they work. Provide assistance as needed.
- Collect their work once they have completed it.
- For the next class, show anonymous examples of good paragraphs and common errors.

UNIT REVIEW

10 MINS

Students can work in groups on this recap of the unit. For questions **2** and **3**, encourage them to check the relevant pages of the unit for answers.

- Allow students time to answer the two questions in groups. For question **1**, ask students to convince the other students in their groups to agree with their choice. Have them justify their reasons.
- Ask each group to present its answer for question **1**. Do they all agree? Why or why not?

SMART ADVICE

ACADEMIC TRACK
Business

ACADEMIC SKILLS

READING	Taking notes (Part 2)
WRITING	Giving details that support advice
GRAMMAR	Using the zero conditional to give advice
CRITICAL THINKING	Applying an idea to a new context

UNIT OVERVIEW

The theme of this unit is advice. It explores the different ways that three entrepreneurs—Banks, Andrade, and Kawasaki—have been able to make a success out of their visionary ideas.

- **READING 1:** The reading is about Ken Banks, a social entrepreneur, and his creation of FrontlineSMS. Banks gives advice on starting entrepreneurial projects.

- **VIDEO:** The video provides a description of Martín Andrade's project, Mi Parque, which creates green spaces in poor, urban areas of Chile.

- **READING 2:** The reading passage describes the lessons that Guy Kawasaki has learned from working in the business world, many of which he learned from Steve Jobs, his boss at Apple.

Students draw on what they've read and watched about advice and success to write an advice paragraph about succeeding in college. The unit prepares them by introducing vocabulary to talk about advice, explaining how to use the zero conditional, and offering tips on how to write an advice paragraph. Students will also learn a new method for taking notes. Lastly, students brainstorm and use an outline to prepare drafts.

THINK AND DISCUSS (page 183)
5 MINS

The questions help prepare students for the subject matter covered in the unit— advice and what they have learned. The scene depicts Sheryl Sandberg, Chief Operating Officer of Facebook, delivering a commencement speech at Tsinghua University, China.
- Have students study the picture, title, and captions.

- Discuss the photo as a class. What do students think the photo and the unit are about? Provide your own overview.
- Discuss the two questions as a class. Ask students to reflect on their own lives. For question **1**, ask who gave them this advice. For question **2**, ask if their school has a career counselor.

ANSWER KEY

THINK AND DISCUSS

Answers will vary. Possible answers:

1. You have to enjoy the little things in life.
2. I would talk to Professor Chumley. She's a person that I trust, and she knows me well.

EXPLORE THE THEME (pages 184–185)
15 MINS

Students read the information and the chart about jobs that show potential for growth in the future.
- Allow students time to study the spread and answer question **1** individually.
- Have students discuss questions **1** and **2** in pairs.
- Discuss answers as a class.
- Have students answer the question in part **B** in pairs.
- Elicit example sentences from students for each of the blue words.

p. 184

ANSWER KEY

EXPLORE THE THEME

A   Answers will vary. Possible answers:

1. I would like to be a translator because I love languages, but I'll have to work on my language skills for that! Being a personal shopper would be fun too, because I like shopping and giving advice.

2. I think these job opportunities are increasing because these jobs can't be done using machines or a computer. They require human input.

B   thoroughly; challenge; expertise

Reading 1

PREPARING TO READ (page 186)

A Building Vocabulary

Students find the seven blue words in the passage and use contextual clues to guess the meanings. Before they begin, ask students to underline the words that they already know and circle the ones that they need to learn.

- Allow time for students to complete the exercise individually.
- Check answers as a class. What clues from the reading passage did students find helpful?
- Elicit example sentences for each vocabulary item. Ask: How do companies *promote* their products? When working on a group project, do you usually take the *initiative*? If runners want to *monitor* their progress, what can they do?

See Vocabulary Extension 10A on page 212 of the Student Book for additional practice with Word Partners: Expressions with challenge.

B Using Vocabulary

Students should practice using the new vocabulary items while answering the three questions.

- Have students discuss their answers in pairs.
- Compare answers as a class. Elicit example answers from students. For question **1**, ask: In the future, what would you like your area of *expertise* to be? For question **2**, ask: Do you enjoy *challenges*? Why or why not? For question **3**, ask: How do teachers try to *empower* students?

C Brainstorming

Students think about what areas of their life would be most affected if they didn't have Internet access.

- Have students work individually to complete the exercise. Ask them to keep their answers brief.
- Have them compare answers in pairs.
- Create a word web on the board, and elicit answers from different pairs in the class.

D Predicting

Students skim the first and last paragraphs and look at the pictures and captions to complete the sentence with their ideas about the reading.

- Have students work individually. Give them a time limit of 1 to 2 minutes to skim the material.
- Have them form pairs and compare answers.
- Discuss ideas with the class. Revisit answers after students have read the passage.

PREPARING TO READ

A 1. exchange (Note: *Exchange* is a verb as well as a noun.)
2. Reality
3. monitor (Note: *Monitor* is a verb as well as a noun.)
4. Funding
5. promote
6. empower
7. initiative

B Answers will vary. Possible answers:
1. I love English and history. English is my area of expertise.
2. public speaking; I overcame this through hard work and practice—the more often I spoke in class or in large groups, the easier it became.
3. A manager can listen carefully to what employees tell them. A manager can give employees more responsibility, more freedom, and adequate training to learn new skills.

C Answers will vary. Possible answers: social life; work; banking; travel planning

D Answers will vary. Possible answers: I think Ken Banks created an app that helps millions of people who live in rural areas and have no Internet access.

🎧 **2.09** Have students read the passage individually, or play the audio and have students read along.

OVERVIEW OF THE READING

The reading passage is about Ken Banks, a social entrepreneur, who noticed that people in developing countries did not have access to the Internet. He created FrontlineSMS, a worldwide service that allows users to connect their cell phones to their computers to communicate. Ken Banks also gives advice to aspiring entrepreneurs.

Online search terms: FrontlineSMS; Ken Banks TED talk; Kiwanja.net

A Understanding the Main Idea

Students are asked to choose the best alternative title for the reading passage. Direct students' attention to the footnote, explaining the meaning of *entrepreneur*. Ask whether they know any entrepreneurs. Then elicit the meaning of *developing country* (a poor country trying to become wealthier and more socially advanced).

- Have students complete the activity individually.
- Check answers as a class. Ask students how they arrived at their answers.

B Understanding Details

Students test their understanding of the details in the passage by answering the questions.

- Allow students time to complete the questions individually.
- Have them form pairs and compare their answers.
- Check answers as a class.

C Identifying Sequence

Have students sequence the steps according to the reading passage.

- Have students form pairs and compare answers.
- Check answers as a class. Ask students if they think these steps would be easy to follow. Why or why not?

D Critical Thinking: Applying an Idea to a New Context

The *Critical Thinking* box points out that using new information in another context can help to evaluate the pros and cons of that idea. Explain that students can try to develop their ideas by completing the following sentences: "This idea would be good because…"; "It might be difficult because…"; "This would help…"

- Have students think about what they have read and discuss their ideas in groups of three or four.
- Discuss answers as a class.

E Critical Thinking: Inferring

Have students read the quote and discuss its implications.

- Have students discuss their answers in pairs.
- Discuss as a class. Elicit the meaning of *crowdsourcing/crowdfunding*, and remind students that they learned about this topic in Unit 3.

UNDERSTANDING THE READING

A a

B Answers will vary. Possible answers:

1. He noticed that many villagers in South Africa had cell phones. (See Paragraph B.)
2. FrontlineSMS is free and can work almost anywhere in the world. (See Paragraph D.)
3. in Malawi—to run a rural healthcare program; in Nigeria—to monitor elections; in Haiti—to help disaster relief efforts. (See Paragraph D.)
4. **a.** Research your idea or product thoroughly.
   b. Promote your idea on social media.
   c. Once the message is out, ask for funding.

C 5, 4, 2, 3, 1

D Answers will vary. Possible answers:

1. Scientists could send texts giving advice on how to help the animal. Members of the public could also send texts to report sightings of that animal.
2. Teachers could send texts containing reading material and questions, and the children could reply if they have queries.

   I think FrontlineSMS would be more useful for protecting endangered animals because it's hard for children to learn via text. They do better in a classroom.

E Answers will vary. Possible answer: I think this is because the Internet has made global communication possible. Because of social media, information about a new product can go viral very quickly.

 **DEVELOPING READING SKILLS** *(page 190)*

Reading Skill: Taking Notes (Part 2)

The *Reading Skill* box describes how to take notes by identifying the main ideas and supporting details. Have a volunteer read the text in the box aloud. Then have students work in pairs, and have one student go to page 8 and one to page 28. Have them summarize the material and report to their partners.

A Taking Notes

Students should complete the chart with the information from the reading passage. Have a student read the examples aloud. Encourage students to use abbreviations where possible.

- Allow time for students to complete the task in pairs.
- Compare notes as a class. Draw the chart on the board, and write answers that volunteers offer.

B Applying

Students use their notes in exercise **A** to write a summary paragraph. Remind students that they learned about writing summaries in Unit 9.

- Have students write paragraphs individually.
- Have them form pairs and compare their paragraphs.
- Ask for volunteers to read their paragraphs to the class.

ANSWER KEY

DEVELOPING READING SKILLS

A   Answers will vary. Possible answers:

Paragraph C. Main Idea: how FrontlineSMS works. **Details:** Users install software; connect computer to cell phone, etc.

Paragraph D. Main Idea: Frontline = free/helps people around the world. **Details:** Examples: helps update medical records in Malawi; monitor elections in Nigeria; disaster relief in Haiti.

Paragraph F. Main Idea: Don't ask for money right away because you need to know it's a good idea. **Details:** Donors want to see well-researched ideas. Talk to consumers.

Paragraph G. Main Idea: Promote your idea using the Internet. **Details:** Use social media: Facebook/Twitter/blogs. Connect online. Post a lot.

Paragraph H. Main Idea: After you have a good idea & promote it, ask for money. **Details:** Start with your social networks. Waiting shows that you have commitment and initiative.

B   Answers will vary. Possible answers:

While living in South Africa in 2003 and 2004, Ken Banks got the idea for a computer program called FrontlineSMS. It allows people to …

Video

VIEWING: THE COMMUNITY BUILDER *(pages 191–192)*

Overview of the Video

The video describes the work of Martín Andrade, who created the organization Mi Parque in order to bring green spaces to poor, urban areas of Chile. He also gives advice to those who wish to organize projects in their own communities.

Online search terms: National Geographic Chile; Martín Andrade Green Spaces; why do green spaces matter

BEFORE VIEWING

A Learning about the Topic

> C The Idea
> D Free & works anywhere
> F Research before asking for money
> G. Promote it
> H Funding
>
> 0 059181

BEFORE VIEWING

A   Answers will vary. Possible answers:

1. Public spaces in poorer areas were dirty and ugly.

2. to improve the lives of low-income Chilean families

3. The foundation will build more green parks.

B 1. found

2. get you down

3. breathtaking

WHILE VIEWING

A ▶ Understanding Main Ideas

Have students read the items silently before you play the video. Then have the students watch the video and check the items that are discussed. Elicit the meanings of *a lack of* (not enough) and to *impact* (affect). Ask how these words might relate to the video.

- Have students complete the task while the video is playing.
- Have students compare answers in pairs.
- Check answers as a class. Ask students whether they remember any details about the topics discussed.

B ▶ Understanding Details

Have students fill in any answers that they recall from the first viewing before playing the video a second time.

- Have students complete the task while the video is playing.
- Have them form pairs and compare answers.
- Check answers as a class. Ask students if there are any other words that they need to have explained, and elicit definitions from volunteers.

P192

P192

ANSWER KEY

WHILE VIEWING

A   2, 3 (Note: The video mentions that Andrade is an architect, but it doesn't go into any detail about how his career began.)

B   Answers will vary. Possible answers:
  1. lack of funding
  2. 30,000 volunteers joined the efforts
  3. **a.** Start small.
     b. Use social media to promote your foundation.

AFTER VIEWING

A Reacting to the Video

Students should discuss the question based on the information they have learned in the video and their own ideas. First, elicit descriptions of the "before and after" footage of the area in Chile. Ask students to imagine how they would feel, volunteering for this effort and enjoying the park afterward.

- Have students discuss the question in pairs.
- Discuss as a class. Make a list of ideas on the board.

B Critical Thinking: Synthesizing

Students reflect on the quote. Then they draw on information from the video and readings in this textbook (including earlier units) to discuss "simple things" that can make a difference. First, have students paraphrase what Andrade is saying. Then encourage them to flip through the textbook and take notes. You may want to congratulate students on completing so much of the textbook. This is an opportunity to reflect on how much content they have learned as a class.

- Allow students time to answer the question individually.
- Have students form pairs and compare their ideas.
- Discuss as a class. Elicit examples and write them on the board. Ask: Do you participate in any of these activities already? If so, which one(s)? If not, would you like to be part of any?

Ideas for… EXPANSION

Have students discuss the green spaces in the area where the school is located. Imagine that they have a meeting with a city planner. What advice would they give to the city planner? Have them work in groups to think of suggestions. Show a map of the area for them to work with, if one is available. Then have students role-play an encounter between the city planner and the mayor, who might be worried about money.

P.192

P.192

ANSWER KEY

AFTER VIEWING

A   Answers will vary. Possible answers: Kids are able to play safely and have fun; older people can take a stroll and improve their health; neighbors can gather outdoors and strengthen community bonds; everyone can breathe fresher air. It's easier to relax when you have green spaces around you.

B   Answers will vary. Possible answers:
  1. Just smiling and opening doors for strangers can improve people's moods and help make the world a better place.
  2. The windmill invention in Unit 2 is a relatively simple invention using recycled materials. That definitely helps make the world a better place!
  3. Not eating big fish (Unit 4) is a simple thing that we can do to help restore the ocean's biodiversity.

P.32

P.32

Reading 2

PREPARING TO READ (page 193)

30 MINS

A Building Vocabulary

Students find the eight blue words in the passage and use contextual clues to guess the meanings. Before they begin, ask students to underline the words that they already know and circle the ones that they need to learn.

- Have students complete the exercise individually.
- Check answers as a class. Elicit example sentences for each vocabulary item. Ask: What is something you are *passionate* about? What is the *reputation* of your local sports teams? Do you think you are a demanding *consumer*?

See Vocabulary Extension 10B on page 212 of the Student Book for additional practice with Word Partners: Expressions with quality.

B Using Vocabulary

Students should use the new vocabulary items while discussing the three questions.

- Have students work in pairs to answer the questions.
- Discuss answers as a class. Elicit example answers from students. Ask volunteers to share what have been the *defining* moments in their own lives. Ask students if they own any items from the brands they mention. Do they agree that the *quality* is excellent? Ask students whether they think of themselves as *sensible*. Why or why not?

C Predicting

Students scan the reading passage by focusing on lessons that Kawasaki has learned. Elicit that students should look for words such as *lesson* and *learn*, and read the first sentence of each paragraph.

- Students should write their answers individually. Give students 1 minute to find this information.
- Have students form pairs and compare answers.
- Have students discuss answers as a class. Revisit these ideas after reading.

P. 193

2.10 Have students read the passage individually, or play the audio and have students read along.

OVERVIEW OF THE READING

The reading passage describes the lessons that Guy Kawasaki has learned over his years working for companies, including Apple, where he promoted the Macintosh computer with Steve Jobs as his boss. He talks about important lessons that he has learned and gives advice for using social media.

Online search terms: Guy Kawasaki; TED Talk Simon Sinek; Steve Jobs speech

UNDERSTANDING THE READING *(page 196)*

40 MINS

A Understanding the Main Idea

Students read the passage and then choose the main purpose from three options.

- Allow time for students to complete the task individually.
- Check answers as a class. Ask students how they arrived at their answers.

B Identifying Opinions

Students read the statements and decide which ones Kawasaki agrees with or disagrees with based on the information in the reading passage. If the topic was not discussed in the reading passage, students should circle NG for *not given*. If students finish early, have them rewrite the statements so that Kawasaki would agree with them.

- Allow time for students to complete the task individually.
- Have students check answers in pairs.
- Check answers as a class. Ask students if they agree with these statements.

C Critical Thinking: Inferring Meaning

Students read the passage again to find the meanings of the words and phrases from the context. Point out that some are examples of figurative language.

- Allow students time to answer the questions individually.
- Check answers with the class. Have students use these words in example sentences. Ask: What has been a *turning point* in your life? How do you know when a business has *taken off*? What is an example of what someone might do that could *burn bridges*? What is a relationship that often involves *power struggles*?

D Critical Thinking: Synthesizing

Students reflect on the advice given in the two readings and the video. They should discuss similarities and differences.

- Allow students time to flip through the unit and make short notes.
- Have students discuss the question in pairs.
- Discuss as a class. Ask students which advice they find the most useful.

harry Potter

UNDERSTANDING THE READING

A   C

B 1. N (See Paragraph B.)
   2. N (See Paragraph F.)
   3. Y (See Paragraph G.)
   4. NG
   5. Y (See Paragraph H.)
   6. N (See Paragraph I.)
   7. Y (See the sidebar "Selling a Product.")

C 1. power struggle
   2. turning point
   3. philosophy
   4. clueless
   5. take off
   6. burn your bridges

D   Answers will vary. Possible answers:

Similarities: All three men are successful and passionate about what they do. They work hard; are entrepreneurs; use social media a lot; don't give up easily; and have identified solutions to problems. Also, Banks and Andrade talk about funding.

Differences: Andrade and Banks are social entrepreneurs and focus on helping people in developing countries, while Kawasaki works mainly for big businesses and brands. Andrade asks for help from local volunteers, but Banks and Kawasaki don't mention this.

Ideas for… **EXPANSION**

Explain to students that in the United States, during university commencement speeches, it is typical for well-known and successful people to give advice to graduating students. There are many great speeches, including the commencement speeches by Steve Jobs, J. K. Rowling, Oprah Winfrey, Jim Carrey, Sheryl Sandberg, and Barack Obama. Have students take a class vote on whose speeches they want to watch. After choosing two or three speeches, watch them together. (The speeches can be found online by using the celebrity's name and *commencement speech*.) Have students take notes on what they learn and then discuss the advice as a class.

Writing

OVERVIEW

In this section, students prepare to write paragraphs that give advice. The lesson starts by teaching students how to use the zero conditional. Students then learn how to write details that support advice. In the *Writing Task*, students apply these lessons by brainstorming, planning, and writing about advice. As added support, they will encounter two drafts of sample paragraphs and revising strategies that the author used. Students will use a checklist to revise their own paragraphs. Editing practice helps students correct common mistakes with the zero conditional. After this, students write the final drafts of their paragraphs.

EXPLORING WRITTEN ENGLISH *(pages 197–199)*

A Noticing

Students read sentences and decide whether the underlined clause shows a condition or a result. This exercise is to be done before going over the information in the *Language for Writing* box. Elicit that *if* clauses are used to show a condition that causes something else to happen.

• Have students complete the task individually.
• Check answers as a class. Ask volunteers to read the sentences aloud.

Language for Writing: Using the Zero Conditional to Give Advice

The *Language for Writing* box describes how to use the zero conditional. It explains that each conditional sentence has a condition (the *if* clause) and a result. With the zero conditional, both clauses have verbs in the present tense. However, the clauses can have the present tense forms of modal verbs or imperatives. Have students read the text in the box aloud. Have them look again at exercise **A** and indicate whether the sentences have modal verbs or imperatives. Ask them to circle the clauses that have commas and remind them of the rule.

B Language for Writing

Students match the conditions with results.
• Allow students time to complete the activity individually.
• Have them check answers in pairs.
• Check answers as a class.

C Language for Writing

Students create their own sentences using the information in exercise **B** and the zero conditional. You may want to offer the first sentence as an example. Refer students to the *Language for Writing* box on page 197 if they need a more detailed explanation.
• Allow students time to complete the task individually.
• Compare and correct the sentences on the board as a class.

D Language for Writing

Students read the statements, circle the condition, and underline the result. Then they combine the information using the zero conditional. You may want to offer the first sentence as an example.
• Allow students time to complete the task individually.
• Check answers in pairs.
• Compare and correct the sentences on the board as a class. For each sentence, elicit why it would not be logical to have the condition and result clauses reversed.

See Grammar Summary on page 223 of the Student Book for additional practice with using the zero conditional to give advice.

Ideas for... EXPANSION

Have students give advice using the zero conditional. Before class, prepare enough papers for a 2:1 ratio in the class. Write a **problem** at the top of each page. Examples: *I can't sleep at night; My house is too noisy for me to study; I want to meet new people; I have a crush on a girl who doesn't notice me.* (Include this last one only if it is culturally appropriate.) Explain to students that they should write a zero conditional sentence giving advice at the bottom of the page. Then they should fold the paper so that their sentence is hidden. In pairs, have students write advice, fold the paper with the advice on it, and then pass the paper to another group. The new group should not look at the previous advice; they should write their own, fold it, and pass it to a new group. Model this before students begin. After students have written advice on five or six papers, collect the papers, unfold them, and read the statements aloud to the class or post the papers around the class. Vote on the best advice.

EXPLORING WRITTEN ENGLISH

A   b

LANGUAGE FOR WRITING

B   **1.** c; **2.** d; **3.** b; **4.** a

C   **1.** If you need money for college fees, (you should) get a part-time job.

    2. You should/can talk to a career counselor if you want to apply for an internship.

    3. If you want to find the right college, (you should) visit lots of campuses.

    4. You shouldn't simplify things for employees if you want your business to succeed.

D   **1.** Talk to your teacher if <u>you don't understand your homework assignment</u>.

    2. If <u>you can't afford to pay for college</u>, you can apply for a scholarship.

    3. If <u>you can't decide on a college major,</u> take time to try out different classes.

    4. You should talk to your manager if <u>you have a problem with another employee</u>.

Writing Skill: Giving Details that Support Advice

The *Writing Skill* box explains that details about how and why things are important should be provided in a paragraph giving advice. The *Writing Skill* box teaches students to add these details to support their ideas. Have students read the text in the *Writing Skill* box aloud. Ask: Based on this information, what is a mentor? Do you agree with this advice? Why or why not?

E Writing Skill

Students read the paragraph and indicate what kind of information the detail provides by labeling it as *how* or *why*. You may want to offer the first detail as an example.

- Allow students time to complete the task individually.
- Have students check answers in pairs
- Check answers as a class.

F Writing Skill

Students read the ideas, then find the *how* or *why* details in the reading passage. Encourage students to use their own words. Explain that for question **4**, the *how* sentence is what companies should do.

- Have students complete the task individually.
- Have students check their answers in pairs.
- Check answers as a class. Ask students whether they agree with this advice.

WRITING SKILL

E   a, b, b, a, b, a

F   Answers will vary. Possible answers:

    1. Customers often don't know what they want/need until they see it. (See Paragraph F.)

    2. If a product looks good, consumers will be more likely to buy it, even if the price is high. (See Paragraph G.)

    3. Employees do their best work when they are given big goals or challenges. (See Paragraph H.)

    4. *Why:* Most experts are disconnected from customers.

      How: Companies should reach out to customers directly, via social media. (See Paragraph I.)

WRITING TASK   *(page 200)*

A Brainstorming

Remind students that brainstorming is a useful first step for gathering ideas before writing. Read the text in the *Goal* box aloud so students will be familiar with the writing task before brainstorming. Provide one or two example ideas. Ideas should be briefly worded. They need not be listed in any order.

- Allow time for students to think about the task individually. Provide assistance as needed.
- Have students brainstorm their ideas in pairs and offer feedback to each other.

B Planning

Have students follow steps 1 to 4 to write an advice paragraph. Have a student read the steps aloud. Remind students that complete sentences are not necessary.

- Allow time for students to complete their outlines individually. Provide assistance as needed.

C First Draft

Have students write first drafts of their paragraphs based on their outlines.

- Allow time for students to complete the task individually. Provide assistance as needed. Refrain from error correction at this point.

WRITING TASK

A Answers will vary. Possible answers:

Topic: how to make friends in college

Tips: Smile a lot and listen to others. Join clubs or sports teams. Spend time just "hanging out." Attend school-related events.

B Answers will vary. Possible answers:

Topic Sentence: Making friends is an important part of college life, and there are some ways to make this easier.

Supporting Idea (Tip 1): Smile a lot and listen to others.

Detail(s): You don't have to be the life of the party; just let people see that you are friendly and approachable.

Supporting Idea (Tip 2): Join clubs or sports teams.

Detail(s): You can meet people who have the same interests as you.

Supporting Idea (Tip 3): Spend time "hanging out" with other students in your dorm or after class.

Detail(s): Friendships take time! It takes time to get to know people well.

Concluding Sentence: This advice can help students make friends in college.

REVISING PRACTICE *(page 201)*

The *Revising Practice* box contains an exercise that demonstrates several ways students can improve their first drafts.

- Allow time for students to analyze the two drafts and complete the exercise.
- Check answers as a class. Ask students to identify each change and explain how it makes the revised draft stronger.

D Revised Draft

Students should apply the revision techniques used in the *Revising Practice* box to their own drafts, where applicable.

- Explain to students that they will be using the questions as a guide for checking and improving their drafts.
- As a class, go over the questions carefully to make sure students understand them.
- Allow students time to revise their paragraphs.

EDITING PRACTICE *(page 202)*

The *Editing Practice* box trains students to spot and correct common errors related to zero conditionals. As a class, go over the information in the box carefully.

- Allow students time to complete the exercise individually.
- Have students check answers in pairs.
- Check answers as a class by asking students to read their corrected sentences aloud and explain the errors.

REVISING PRACTICE

b, a, d, d, c

EDITING PRACTICE

1. If you want to make new friends in <u>college, attend</u> as many school-related events as you can.

2. If you <u>want</u> to find out if a particular college is right for you, visit the campus before classes start.

3. You can apply for a <u>scholarship if</u> you don't have enough money for college.

4. If you plan to ask your boss for a raise, you should <u>write</u> a list of your recent accomplishments at work.

5. You can get a bank <u>loan if</u> you don't have enough money to start a business.

6. If you want your employees to feel empowered, <u>make</u> sure that they have the necessary resources and expertise to do their jobs.

E Final Draft

Have students apply the skills taught in *Editing Practice* to their own revised drafts and check for any other errors.

- Allow time for students to work individually on editing their drafts.
- Walk around and monitor students as they work. Provide assistance as needed.
- Collect their work once they have completed it.
- For the next class, show anonymous examples of good paragraphs and common errors.

⏱ 10 MINS UNIT REVIEW

Students can work in groups on this recap of the unit. For question **1**, encourage students to explain their reasons. For questions **2** and **3**, encourage them to check the relevant pages of the unit for answers.

- Allow students time to answer the three questions in groups. For question **1**, ask groups if they think they will give this advice to other people. Why or why not?
- As a class, have students vote for the best piece of advice.

UNIT 1 Longevity Leaders

Narrator: The elderly are found across all countries and cultures. And their numbers are increasing as people live longer.

There are over seven billion people in the world today. And this number could reach nine billion by the year 2050. There will be more elderly in the world than ever before. We will see aging populations all over the world in the 21st century.

Andrew Zolli: In places like the United States, Europe, even China, we see populations that are getting much older much faster.

Narrator: But how old is old?

In the natural world, there are animals that live for centuries. Some researchers believe that some whales can live for 200 years or more. Giant tortoises are known to live for 150 years or more. Elephants are known to live for up to 70 years.

Humans live longer than most animals. They can live to a maximum of about 120 years. Of course, most humans don't live that long. But there are places in the world where people live longer—and healthier—lives.

This is Sardinia, an island off the coast of Italy. It has a very high number of centenarians. These are people who live to see their 100th birthday. One example is Antonio Bruno, who was still healthy and happy at 103 years old.

Japan also has a very high number of centenarians. The secret to longevity may be found on the Japanese island of Okinawa, where people live longer and healthier lives than anywhere else in the world.

In some ways, centenarians in Okinawa and Sardinia have similar lifestyles, even if their cultures are different. They tend to stay active and eat locally grown food. They have hobbies, like this Okinawan woman who works in her garden every day. Most centenarians also have access to good medical care, and they have the support of their friends and family.

These centenarians seem to be very healthy—but how much longer will such healthy lifestyles last? Younger people are eating more processed foods, and may be less active than their parents and grandparents. With increasing globalization, these traditional lifestyles are fast disappearing.

People today are turning to medical science to help live longer lives. Some scientists have started to treat aging as a disease instead of a natural part of human life.

For now, though, there are few centenarians like this 102-year-old in the world. However, if we follow their example—eat healthy, stay active, and keep our families close—then we may see more centenarians in our future. And our future may be very long indeed.

UNIT 2 Solar Solutions

Narrator: This is the Egypt familiar to most people. Cairo is a big, busy city. But there's a whole other world up here, high on the city's rooftops.

Many Egyptians use the space on rooftops for water tanks, satellite dishes, and even livestock. The garbage piled everywhere is considered valuable because it's often recycled and reused. Cairo has been "going green" long before it became fashionable.

That's why National Geographic Emerging Explorer Thomas Taha Culhane's program has been so special. He's been helping lower-income Egyptians build solar-powered water heaters—partly out of recycled trash—and putting them on their rooftops.

Thomas Culhane: People will come to this community, and they'll look on the rooftops and they'll say why is there so much trash on the roofs, but if you talk to the homeowners they'll say, "What trash? I'm saving this for the future when I can figure out a good way to use it." So there is no trash. And that is, I think, the message that inner-city Cairo, and the informal communities of Cairo, have for the world. Forget this idea that there is garbage. One man's garbage is another's gold mine.

Narrator: The water heaters take advantage of Egypt's great national resource—abundant sunshine. When the system is placed just right …

Culhane: Oh, you're good. You are good. You know what you're at? 39.9 degrees. Whoa. Whoa.

Narrator: Solar panels heat up water that circulates through metal tubes, eventually filling a tank with extremely hot water.

Culhane: This is a hand-made solar hot water system, and it's made out of local community materials, recycled materials, and even some garbage. And we put it together as cheaply as possible to demonstrate that anybody can make a solar hot water system; that renewable energy is not some exotic technology; that it can be made from found materials and it works.

Narrator: The solar heaters allow urban dwellers access to a plentiful supply of hot water. The heaters improve the quality of life and sanitation, and they cut down on potential energy costs. Culhane says the only problem is the dust from the nearby desert that coats the city and the panels.

Culhane: Solar works tremendously well if there's sun. Cairo has sun. But it also has dust. Until people appreciate that, they won't come up and just do the simple thing of just wiping the dust away. So really it's a matter of just a few seconds to wipe it down and then the system is functioning again. But because people don't do this, they will say, "Solar does not work in Cairo." And what we have to do is get them to be as aware of the need to just dust these as they are dusting their kitchen table. Once they accept that, solar is a no-brainer here. It's an easy thing to do.

Narrator: Culhane hopes the water heater project will lead to other innovations using recycled materials. As the saying goes, one man's garbage is another man's treasure.

UNIT 3 Citizen Scientists

Dr. Fredrik Hiebert: The Burkhan Khaldun, it's not just a mountain. It's a whole mountain range. It's more than 12,000 square kilometers. To begin to investigate that area, it would take more than 100 archaeologists all their lives just to begin to look.

Dr. Albert Lin: So we're asking the public to scan the entire area through the human computation network and tell us where to go so we can find any possible traces of Burkhan Khaldun.

Narrator: To find the tomb of Genghis Khan, Dr. Lin's team use what they call a "human computation network." The team shared 85,000 satellite images of the region on their website. Citizen scientists around the world scan the images and tag anything that looks unusual. Some of these might be ancient structures.

Dr. Lin: This is the data that just came in today, huh?

Member of team: Mm-hmm. These are the most recent tags that have been uploaded onto the data pads.

Dr. Lin: Hundreds of our citizen scientists tagged this unusual rectangle shape on the satellite map. Straight lines are usually a good indicator that something's man-made. The site is less than two miles from our camp. Could it be the tomb of Genghis Khan? We're going to go check it out.

We're going to scan every single one of the human computation sites that have been picked out on that mountain and try to figure out what people saw.

Narrator: Lin and his team get on horses and ride out to the site. There, they find something interesting.

Dr. Lin: We come upon this thing, this thing that was identified by the public, made of rocks sticking out of the earth. This is it. Whoa, cool!

Dr. Hiebert: It's clearly a tomb, but it's too old to be Genghis Khan's. It's Bronze Age, it's more than 3,000 years old.

Dr. Lin: Well, you can see this is a very well-structured rectangular shape, these rocks set up like a home, you know. And the opening there represents a door, and always the door is facing south, so south is directly that way. I mean, if people hundreds of miles away can guide us through satellite images to this ancient grave site, then I feel like we've got a chance to find the tomb of Genghis Khan.

UNIT 4 Saving Bluefin Tuna

Narrator: Japanese scientist Shukei Masuma is on a mission. He is trying to save the bluefin tuna from becoming extinct. Their numbers have declined significantly over the last decade, largely due to overfishing.

Masuma's solution? To breed them in captivity. He feeds the tuna himself. Here, he visits the huge pools where adults are separated from the young. Says Masuma: "I'm realizing more and more how difficult it is to uncover knowledge about the bluefin. At this point, I'm relying on all my strength and energy."

When evening comes, he waits at the edge of the pool. He hopes to see the beginning of bluefin life. Once the big fish have laid their eggs, Masuma slowly puts the eggs into special tanks. From this stage on, he will take care of them. His goal is to keep them alive until they are old enough to be returned to the sea. He hopes his tuna will grow large enough to breed in the wild.

It's a difficult job. Many hatchlings, or baby fish, do not survive. But after years of hard work, Masuma has found a stable temperature and the right food for his hatchlings. Now he is able to breed them in large numbers. He shows ocean scientist Sylvia Earle how life begins for these giant fish.

Sylvia Earle: Already you see the eyes. Is that what these are—the eyes beginning to form?

Shukei Masuma: Eyes, they have formed … and heart is beating, of course.

Earle: Masuma, you were the first to actually pull off this great miracle.

Masuma: Thank you very much.

Narrator: Someday, Masuma will send these hatchlings back into the ocean. There, they will hopefully have a positive effect on the population. But first they have to avoid getting caught.

Scientists estimate that the bluefin tuna population in the Atlantic Ocean is now only one-fifth of its population in the 1970s. And their numbers have dramatically decreased in the Mediterranean Sea and the Pacific Ocean.

The future for the species does not look good. Unless we greatly reduce the number of fish we catch each year, these giants of the sea will eventually die out.

UNIT 5 House of Cards

Nelson Dellis: My name is Nelson Dellis, and I'm the 2011 USA Memory Champion.

To sum up, basically what I do to memorize a deck of cards in simple steps, the first is I code each card in a deck to someone familiar, with an associated action, and an associated object.

The next step is I group three cards at a time. The first card is always a person, the second card is an action, and the third card is an object. So I basically make this little story of a person doing something with an object. So it's kind of like the game Clue, almost. I'm making this, you know, who did what with what.

The next step is I place that image around [a] familiar mental map in my mind.

So at the 2011 USA Memory Championship, the particular deck of cards that I memorized, I could still remember. I decided to choose my girlfriend's apartment. So if you walk to the first room, you can see the first three cards grouped together, which is a horse running around with Harry Potter's wand. To me, that translates to five of diamonds, that's the horse; running around is eight of spades; and then the four of clubs is Harry Potter, but his object is a wand.

OK, so if we walk around the corner from the bathroom, we're in kind of this hallway area, and there's my ex-girlfriend swallowing a sword. Ace of clubs is my ex-girlfriend; queen of spades is the action of swallowing something; and seven of diamonds is a sword.

Through the balcony, through the bedroom, and then to the bathroom, we have Arnold Schwarzenegger dancing with a car. So Arnold Schwarzenegger is ace of spades; dancing, the action of dancing, is queen of clubs; and the car is nine of spades.

And then, if we go down outside into the lobby, you'll see my former boss dropping a Rubik's Cube. The seven of hearts is, is her. Two of spades is Britney Spears, and her action is always saying "Oops, I did it again," like in her song—to me that's dropping something. Ace of diamonds is me, and I'm a big fan of doing the Rubik's Cube, so my object is the Rubik's Cube.

Karst

UNIT 6 The Frog Licker

Narrator: Off the southeastern coast of Africa lies the island of Madagascar. Madagascar is known for its wide-eyed lemurs, but it also has one of the world's most colorful amphibians—the Mantella poison frog.

Poison frogs aren't born poisonous. Instead, they are proof of the old saying: "You are what you eat." Their toxins are actually a side effect of their diet, which is made up of ants, millipedes, and mites. But which insects, specifically? And will the loss of these insects endanger the frogs?

Meet scientist Valerie C. Clark. Valerie encounters *Mantella betsileo*, a very widespread species of poison frog. This one appears to be carrying eggs.

Valerie Clark: How do I know? Because it's just very, very fat, and this is the season for love.

Narrator: Clark and her colleagues use GPS data to record the frog's location, and other useful information.

Clark: We're right at sea level.

Narrator: They also need to collect as many insects as possible to try to track down exactly what these frogs are eating. First, Valerie's team chops up the leaves, then puts them into mesh bags—ones that have lots of little holes. They hang the bags up inside another bag, with a little plastic bag filled with alcohol attached to the bottom. As the soil dries out inside the mesh bag, the insects escape to find water and fall out. These become their samples.

How do you test the toxins in a frog's skin? There are a couple of methods. One way is to wipe their backs with tissue soaked in alcohol. But another way is what Clark calls the "quick lick" taste test.

Clark: Well, let's see. Oh, it's definitely bitter.

Narrator: Bitterness equals toxic. It seems like a risky thing to do, but Mantella are only mildly toxic to humans. They are brightly colored to warn predators to stay away.

These toxins in the frogs' skin may be harmful to other animals, but may be very valuable to humans. They could be an important contribution to medical science, providing pain relief and cures for diseases.

Clark: By sampling frogs for their toxic chemicals, we're effectively taking a shortcut to the many, many chemicals that exist in countless insects in the rain forest.

Narrator: Back in the village, the results look promising.

Clark: Oh! Here we go! I'm very excited about these samples. This is certainly making up the great portion of the Mantella diet and has great potential to end up being some of the sources of their chemicals.

Narrator: The frogs need to eat many types of insects for their toxins to work. The bigger the forest, the more insects to choose from. If we start cutting down rain forest and affecting the ecosystem, it reduces our chances of finding new drug cures.

Clark: So the more primary forest that we have, the better chance we have of finding new drug leads.

Narrator: Near the end of her journey, Clark has collected 500 tubes of insects. These could lead her to some sources of the frogs' toxins.

The message is clear. In order to save the poison frogs of Madagascar, people will have to save the rain forest with its amazing diversity of insects.

UNIT 7 Lightning

Narrator: A lightning storm. It's an incredible natural event—one that scientists are still learning about.

On hot summer days, it's common to see flashes of lightning in the sky. It's estimated that lightning occurs 50 to 100 times a second around the world. Regions with the most lightning strikes include Central Africa, the Himalayas, and South America.

Lightning is often seen flashing between storm clouds and the earth. These flashes of light are pure electricity. Scientists aren't exactly sure how lightning escapes from the cloud. They think it occurs because of movement of air within rain clouds.

Lighter particles moving toward the top of clouds become positively charged, while heavier particles heading toward the bottom become negatively charged. In conditions where positive and negative charges grow big enough, lightning occurs between these regions.

Most lightning occurs within the cloud, but some strike the earth in bright flashes. In these cases, the lightning escapes the cloud and extends toward the ground in a branching pattern, like a tree. Just one lightning strike contains hundreds of millions of volts, and lasts less than a second.

Lightning seems to take the form of a single flash, but it's actually several flashes reaching up into the clouds. Lightning reaches temperatures of more than 28,000 degrees Celsius. This heat causes air around the lightning to expand, which creates the sound of thunder.

In the U.S., lightning occurs most frequently in Florida. Its hot, wet climate is particularly suited for creating thunder clouds.

Lightning kills a significant number of people each year—nearly 100 people on average in the U.S., more than hurricanes or tornadoes.

During thunderstorms, reduce your risk of getting struck by finding shelter inside a building or in vehicles. If caught outside, avoid high ground and isolated trees.

Lightning is a natural and common event, but one that can be deadly.

UNIT 8 A Daring Design

Narrator: Imagine this. It's 1418 in Florence, Italy. You've been challenged to build a great dome for the Santa Maria del Fiore, one of the grandest cathedrals ever built. And you have no formal architectural training. No pressure, right?

For Filippo Brunelleschi, a goldsmith and clockmaker, it was the opportunity of a lifetime. He considered the challenge carefully, then proposed a daring plan, using methods that experts don't fully understand even to this day.

At the time, domes were often built as semicircles. But the town fathers required that Brunelleschi build an eight-sided dome. It would also have no central support system to hold it up during construction. Even worse, the dome's base was an octagon with irregular sides and no true center.

But Brunelleschi knew what to do. There would be two domes instead of one—an inner and an outer shell, connected by brick arches and rings made of stone and wood. The rings would keep the dome from expanding outwards.

Brunelleschi also designed innovative machines to lift heavy materials hundreds of feet up.

Since there was no support system in the center of the dome, the bricks would have to support themselves during construction. To do this, Brunelleschi placed the bricks in an unusual way. He used a herringbone pattern, which ran all the way to the top of the dome, with vertical bricks to hold the others in place.

The builders laid about one row a week, giving the cement time to dry. At this rate, the dome grew very slowly, about a foot a month. But how were the bricks placed so perfectly?

Many experts agree that Brunelleschi used ropes. One theory is that ropes ran from the work platform to the top of the dome to show where the bricks should go. Another theory is that ropes ran from the center, forming cones that grew smaller as they moved to the top. Still another theory suggests that central ropes were used with wooden structures.

However it was done, it worked. The eight sides of the dome met at the top perfectly, just as Brunelleschi had planned.

In all, it took 16 years to complete the dome. When Brunelleschi died in 1446, he left behind no drawings and no details as to exactly how he achieved his masterpiece. Today, it remains the largest brick dome in the world, more than 500 years after it was built.

UNIT 9 Flying Reptiles

Narrator: The paradise tree snake is a special kind of snake. Not because it can climb trees. Many snakes are able to use their rough, overlapping scales to push against tree bark and move upwards.

No. What makes this species so unique is its ability to fly!

These are flying snakes. They fly from tree to tree. In the dense forests of Indonesia, it's the quickest and most efficient way to get from here to there.

First, the snake hangs off the end of the branch in a "J" shape. Then it launches itself, "flying" through the air and down to the ground or another tree. The snake can flatten itself to about twice its normal width. This makes it more of a glider than a flyer. By twisting its flexible body into an "S" shape, the snake can even make turns. This helps the snake cross distances of up to 100 meters.

Other animals have evolved in similar ways. This is the Draco lizard, or "flying dragon." It is prey for the paradise tree snake and other predators of the jungle. The lizard puffs itself up as a warning, but the snake doesn't seem put off by this display.

So the lizard spreads its wings and takes off. These wings are actually thin folds of skin that extend from its body. The Draco uses them to glide from tree to tree, up to 10 meters apart. Like the snake, this ability to "fly" helps it move around the forest quickly and easily.

As for the tree snake, looks like it'll have to find another prey—one that won't escape so easily.

UNIT 10 The Community Builder

Narrator: Chile is a big country. It stretches over 4,300 km along the west coast of South America, and the scenery in many places is breathtaking.

But in some communities there is a lack of green space. In some places there is only 1 square meter of green area per person. Sometimes even less.

But a nonprofit organization called Mi Parque is hoping to change that.

Mi Parque—which translates into "My Park"—was founded by Martín Andrade and a few other architects. The organization aims to create more green space in some of Chile's poorer neighborhoods. So far, Mi Parque has completed over 250 projects and reconstructed nearly 450,000 square meters of park land. But it hasn't been easy.

Martín Andrade: Well, one of our biggest challenges in the beginning was the lack of funding. Many companies didn't want to donate money because they didn't think we would succeed.

Narrator: To deal with this problem, members of Mi Parque asked their friends and family to donate plants, paint, and other construction materials. Using those materials, Mi Parque built its first park. After that, more companies showed an interest and the foundation started to take off.

Andrade: What I'm most proud of is that about 30,000 volunteers from private businesses and local communities have joined our efforts to increase green areas across the country.

Narrator: Andrade's organization has been hugely successful. So what advice would Andrade give to others who want to start a foundation to improve people's lives?

Andrade: First, start small. Don't let the big problems facing society get you down. If you're focused on the resources that you currently have, you'll find that there are simple things that you can do now to make the world a better place.

Also, use social media to promote your foundation. Now, Mi Parque has its own website, Facebook page, and Twitter and Instagram accounts. These social media tools help us to educate the general public about the foundation's goals, and to raise money.

Narrator: Mi Parque's efforts to create more green space have impacted the lives of more than 450,000 people in Chile. But its work is not finished yet. Mi Parque continues to develop green areas throughout the country, in the hope of making green space accessible to everyone.

GRAPHIC ORGANIZERS

Unit 1 Happiness

Complete the T-chart as you read *Is There a Recipe for Happiness?*

SINGAPORE	MEXICO
• The government provides basic needs, e.g., _____ and _____ .	• People spend a lot of time _____ with _____ and _____ .
• There is almost no _____ .	• Most people live near people in a similar _____ .
• Everyone can have a _____ standard of _____ .	• _____ , by itself, may not be that _____ for _____ .
• Streets are generally _____ and people can _____ clean _____ .	• What matters more is how much you have compared to _____ .

Unit 2 Inventive Solutions

Complete the chart as you read *Big Ideas: Little Packages*.

PROBLEMS		SOLUTIONS
Low-birthweight babies don't have much _____, so they often can't keep _____ enough. As a result, they may become so _____ that they _____ .	→	The **Embrace Infant Warmer** looks like a small _____ . It is filled with _____ that heats to a person's usual _____ temperature. It keeps babies _____ without needing _____ to work.
People have to walk many miles to get _____ water for drinking, _____ , and _____ . Often they have to carry it on their _____ in heavy _____ .	→	A **Q Drum** is made of strong _____ material and can store about _____ liters of water. People move it by _____ it over the ground. Anyone, even _____ , can pull the drum using an attached _____ .
Doctors in _____ countries often work in places with no _____ or _____ . They have to send _____ to labs and then wait weeks to receive the _____ .	→	The **health detector** device contains _____ that contain chemicals. When a person puts a drop of _____ on the paper, the chemicals react and change the paper's _____ ; this shows whether or not the person has _____ . Health workers can perform the tests in _____ .

Unit 3 Connected Lives

Complete the summary as you read *Internet Island*.

❶ The Idea

Mark James's new idea was to create an _____ and call it a tribe.

James wanted the _____ tribe to become a real one.

James's idea came from _____ websites. He emailed his friend Ben Keene, who liked the idea.

❷ The Island

Keene and James looked for an _____ for their tribe.

Tui Mali was _____ of a tribe in _____.

He wanted someone to _____ his small island, called _____. He decided to _____ on the Internet.

Keene and James _____ him. They agreed to pay $ _____ for a _____ lease of the island, and $26,500 in _____ to the community. They also promised _____ for the local tribe members.

❸ The New Tribe

In September 2006, Keene and 13 of his tribe members (aged 17 to _____) traveled to the island.

They worked with the local tribe members to put up buildings, plant _____ , and set up clean sources of _____ , such as _____ .

The old and new tribe members became _____ as a result.

❹ The Tribe Keeps Growing

Today, anyone can go to the website to join the _____ tribe, _____ money, or plan _____ .

Since their Vorovoro trip, James and Keene have created other tribal _____ in other parts of the world.

Unit 4 Saving Our Seas

Complete the reporter's notes as you read *What We Eat Makes a Difference: An Interview with Barton Seaver.*

Barton Seaver: a _____ and conservationist who wants us to help him save _____.

He believes people's _____ have a direct effect on the health of the _____. He doesn't believe we should stop _____ altogether—but we should avoid eating certain species that have been _____.

His advice about what to eat:

- We should eat _____ and _____ that are lower on the _____ and can be harvested with little environmental _____ (for example: anchovies, _____, farmed mussels, _____ and oysters, and herring).

- We should not eat _____ fish (like _____, orange roughy, _____, sturgeon, and _____), otherwise these _____ will decline.

He believes that humans are an essential part of _____. He wants us to understand our place on this _____ through the food we eat.

He believes the ocean's health is important to us because the ocean:

- provides most of the _____ we _____.

- has a big effect on the _____ that we rely on for crops and _____.

- provides a necessary and vital _____ for billions of people.

Unit 5 Memory and Learning

Complete the T-chart as you read *The Art of Memory*.

THE ART OF MEMORY: IN THE PAST	THE ART OF MEMORY: NOW
About _____ ago: • Simonides of Ceos invented a powerful memory technique called the _____. • According to the method, if you _____ certain things in a familiar place, you can keep them in your _____ for a long time. • Simonides called this imagined place a _____. In 15th-century Italy: • Peter of Ravenna used this method to _____ books and poems.	In the 20th and 21st centuries: • We've gradually replaced our internal memory with _____ memory. • We've developed new kinds of _____ so we don't have to keep lots of _____ in our _____. For example, we now have: • _____ to record experiences; • _____ for remembering schedules; • computers and the _____ to store our _____.

Unit 6   Animals and Medicine

Complete the chart with situations and results as you read *The Snake Chaser*.

SITUATION	RESULT
Zoltan Tackacs searches for venom components (called _____) that can be used to _____ various _____ .	He has faced many dangerous situations, and survived six venomous _____ . He continues because he wants to make new discoveries.
Animal venoms have been used to develop over a dozen _____ medications.	The drugs can be used to treat high _____ , heart attacks, and other health conditions.
Many drugs produce _____ because they affect more than one _____ in the body.	People may feel sick, suffer from painful _____ , or experience hair loss.
Toxins are able to hit a _____ in the body.	They are a good _____ for new medications.
Finding the right toxin to fight a _____ can take years of work.	New "_____ Toxins" allow for the creation of "toxin libraries."
Designer toxin libraries could eventually hold the _____ of every animal on Earth.	These could help researchers _____ which venom could help _____ a specific disease.
Once a _____ becomes extinct, it is not possible to _____ .	When a venomous animal dies out, it may be that a new drug is _____ , too.

Unit 7 Nature's Fury

Complete the notes with information as you read *When Tornadoes Strike*.

What happened on April 25–28, 2011?	
What happened on April 27, 2011?	
Where do most tornadoes in the United States occur?	
What made the 2011 Tuscaloosa tornado unusual?	
What do experts think caused the tornado outbreak in 2011?	

Unit 8 Building Wonders

Complete the timeline as you read *Unfinished Masterpiece*.

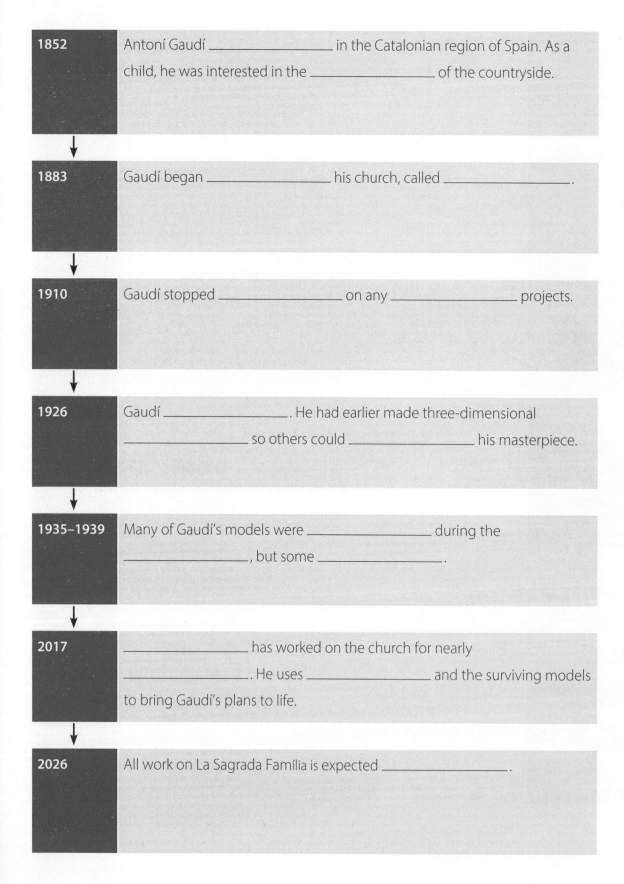

1852 Antoní Gaudí _____ in the Catalonian region of Spain. As a child, he was interested in the _____ of the countryside.

1883 Gaudí began _____ his church, called _____ .

1910 Gaudí stopped _____ on any _____ projects.

1926 Gaudí _____ . He had earlier made three-dimensional _____ so others could _____ his masterpiece.

1935–1939 Many of Gaudí's models were _____ during the _____ , but some _____ .

2017 _____ has worked on the church for nearly _____ . He uses _____ and the surviving models to bring Gaudí's plans to life.

2026 All work on La Sagrada Família is expected _____ .

Unit 9 Form and Function

Complete the information about the animals as you read *Design by Nature*.

Toucan ___bills___

Description	Possible uses	Human applications

Shark _____

Description	Used for	Human applications

Unit 10 Smart Advice

Complete the *Wh-* question chart as you read *Turning Ideas into Reality*.

What was the problem?

Organizations wanted to help _____ communities in _____ but _____ was a big challenge. Many people did not have _____ access.

Who found a solution?

Ken Banks created a new type of computer _____ called FrontlineSMS.

It allows users to send information from without using the Internet.

Why did Banks think Frontline SMS would be successful?

How does Frontline SMS work?

Where has Frontline SMS been used?

What is Banks's advice to entrepreneurs?